Deutsche Presse-Agentur, Hamburg
30 July:

"Reports of NATO mobilisation have been flooding in from all over Europe. The Bundeswehr have mobilised their regular forces and massive troop movements have been observed as Federal units move up to the eastern border. American, British, Dutch, Belgian and Danish troops have also began taking up positions in the Federal Republic.

Along the East German and Czech borders locals report increased activity, mostly at night, as the troops of the Warsaw Pact also muster."

Deutsche Presse-Agentur, Hamburg
4 August:

"War!
Reports are coming in of Soviet forces crossing the border, from Lubeck in the North to the Czech border in the south, and engaging Bundeswehr forces arrayed against them. Initial reports have the Bundeswehr and NATO forces holding their ground."

Hannoversche Allgemeine Zeitung (Hannover General News)
5 August:

"The Federal Government has today issued a statement urging the citizens of Lower Saxony, east of Hannover to evacuate westwards. Various train and bus services have been arranged by the Lower Saxony administration to help evacuate citizens. Ferocious fighting continues along the border regions. People are advised if they find themselves in the combat zone to remain in their basements and to avoid enemy troops."

Erstes Deutsches Fernsehen (First German Television)
10 August:

"I'm here reporting from Ostercappeln on the south bank of the Mitteland Kanal at the Highway 51 crossing. There is a stream of military trucks across the bridge and heading south down Highway 65 towards Osnabrück. I recently spoke to some nearby soldiers, and though they wouldn't give me any details for security reasons, they told me the fight was continuing north of here and NATO will strike back."

U S S R
(UNION OF SOVIET SOCIALIST REPUBLICS)

BLACK SEA

TURKEY

SYRIA

IRAQ

KUWAIT

PERSIAN GULF

LEBANON

JORDAN

SAUDI ARABIA

UAE

ISRAEL

ANEAN

EGYPT

D1307663

TEAM YANKEE
WORLD WAR III

IT'S 1985 AND THE COLD WAR JUST GOT HOT!

Team Yankee is a complete set of rules for playing World War III Wargames.

Based on the book written by Harold Coyle in 1987, Team Yankee brings the conflict that simmered throughout the Cold War to life. You will command your troops in miniature on a realistic battlefield.

In Team Yankee, a heavy combat team of M1 Abrams tanks and M113 armoured personnel carriers faces a Soviet invasion of West Germany. Outnumbered and outgunned, Captain Sean Bannon and his men will have to fight hard and they'll have to fight smart if they are going to survive.

Lt. Colonel Yuri Potecknov's motor rifle battalion is preparing to execute its mission in the scientific manner that he had been taught at the Frunze Military Academy and used in Afghanistan. Victory today will bring the world proletarian revolution that much closer.

Find out more at:

WWW.TEAM-YANKEE.COM

leopard

WEST GERMANS IN WORLD WAR III

Written by: Wayne Turner
Editors: Peter Simunovich, John-Paul Brisigotti
Graphic Design: Casey Davies, Sean Goodison
Assistant Writers: Phil Yates, HW Coyle
Proof Readers: Mark Adelina, Alexander Costantino, Sean Ireland,
Mitch Kemmis, Michael McSwiney, Gary Martin, Luke Parsonage,
Gregg Siter, Stephen Smith, Ken Snell, Garry Wait
Miniatures Design: Evan Allen, Tim Adcock, Matt Bickley, Will Jayne

Cover and Internal Art: Vincent Wai
Miniatures Painting: Aaron Mathie
Web Support: James Brown, George Williams
Playtest Groups: Dad's Army (Gavin Van Rossum),
Northern Battle Gamers (Nigel Slater), Russia (Ilya Grebenkin),
Wardogs Hannover (Kai Bergemann),
M.E.G. Team Voghera (Emilio Arbasino).

Thanks to Jochen Schreiber (Bundeswehr, Ret.)

CONTENTS

All rights reserved. No part of this publication may be reproduced, stored in a retrieval system, or transmitted, in any form or by any means without the prior written permission of the publisher, nor be otherwise circulated in any form of binding or cover other than that in which it is published and without a similar condition being imposed on the subsequent purchaser.

© Copyright Battlefront Miniatures Ltd., 2016. ISBN: 9780994120663

NATO AND WARSAW PACT DEPLOYMENT AND PLANNED WARSAW PACT ATTACKS

Kiel

Lübeck

Wilhelmshaven

Bremerhaven

Hamburg

LANDJUT
xxxx
NORTHAG

1ST NETHERLANDS CORPS

Bremen

xxx

1ST GERMAN CORPS

THE NETHERLANDS

xxx

1ST BRITISH CORPS

Hannover

3RD US CORPS

3RD SHOCK ARMY

Magdeburg

xxx

1ST BELGIUM CORPS

EA

Essen

3RD FRENCH CORPS

Düsseldorf

GROUP O SOVIET FOR IN GERMA (GSFG)

NORTHAG
xxxx
CENTAG

3RD GERMAN CORPS

Cologne

Leipzig

8TH GUARDS ARMY

BONN

WEST GERMANY

xxx

5TH US CORPS

Fulda

Frankfurt

Rhine River

xxx

Saarbrücken

7TH US CORPS

Nürnberg

CENTAG
xxxx
SOUTHAG

FRANCE

1ST FRENCH CORPS

Stuttgart

2ND GERMAN CORPS

2ND FRENCH CORPS

Danube River

Munich

2GUA
TA
AR

2

At the end of World War II (1939 to 1945), the responsibility for the security of Germany was left to the four occupying powers: the United States, Britain, France and the Soviet Union. The relationship between the democratic West (the United States, Britain, and France) and the communist East (the Soviet Union) soon broke down and an 'Iron Curtain' was drawn across central Europe. Germany was divided in two. In 1949, in western Germany, the Federal Republic of Germany *(Bundesrepublik Deutschland)* was formed from the zones occupied by the United States, Britain, and France, and in easterm Germany the German Democratic Republic *(Deutsche Demokratische Republik)* was formed from the Soviet occupied zone. Initially West Germany was forbidden from having a military by the western Allies, but as tension with the Soviets heightened throughout the 1950s, the Allies invited West Germany to join NATO (North Atlantic Treaty Organisation), formed in 1954.

20TH GUARDS ARMY

1ST POLISH ARMY

NORTHERN GROUP OF FORCES (NGF)

POLAND

4TH POLISH ARMY

RLIN

ERMANY

1ST GUARDS TANK ARMY

2ND POLISH ARMY

Dresden

CENTRAL GROUP OF FORCES (CGF)

1ST ECHOSLOVAK MBINED ARMS ARMY

Elbe River

PRAGUE

CZECHOSLOVAKIA

4TH CZECHOSLOVAK COMBINED ARMS ARMY

AUSTRIA

KEY

Each Symbol represents a Division

Armoured Divisions

Armoured Divisions contain between 200 and 350 tanks and 11,000 and 20,000 troops

Mechanised Divisions

Mechanised Divisions contain between 50 and 220 tanks and 13,000 and 20,000 troops

NATO FORCES

United States	
Great Britain	
West Germany	
Belgium & The Netherlands	
France	

WARSAW PACT FORCES

Soviet Union	
Czecho- slovakia	
East Germany	
Poland	

A major reason for West Germany's incorporation into NATO was that without German manpower it would have been impossible to field enough conventional forces to resist a Soviet invasion. In 1950 a committee of former high-ranking *Wehrmacht* (the old German armed forces) Officers was formed to discuss and plan the rebuilding of the German Armed Forces. Former *General der Panzertruppen* of the *Wehrmacht* and liberal politician, Hasso von Manteuffel, suggested the name *Bundeswehr* (Federal Defence) for the new forces, and the name was later agreed to by the West German parliament.

To avoid associating Germany's new military forces with the recent dark history of WWII, a conscious decision was made to shape its traditions on the military reformers of the early 19th century. The *Bundeswehr* was officially formed on 12 November 1955, the 200th birthday of the 19th Century Prussian military reformer Scharnhorst. Over time, the Bundeswehr went on to develop its own traditons.

Bundeswehr personnel were a mix of conscripts and volunteers. Conscripts served for 12 months before returning to civilian life, where they went into the reserve and could be called up in times of crisis or war. These reserves would report to various muster points to be allocated out to bring mobilised units up to strength.

WAR STRATEGY

During the 1960s and 1970s NATO planning revolved around the early use of nuclear weapons against a massive Warsaw Pact attack. Unsurprisingly, the West German government was opposed to any strategy that would leave Germany a radioactive wasteland. There were doubts in NATO, especially among the West Germans, whether conventional combined arms operations could be conducted in nuclear conditions. However, NATO defensive plans continued to rely on nuclear weapons into the 1970s. It wasn't until the mid-1970s that NATO felt there were sufficient conventional ground and air forces in Europe to conduct an effective forward defence without the early use of nuclear weapons.

During the 1970s the *Heer* (the ground forces of the *Bundeswehr*) focused on

defence of the border area with forward-deployed combat units. Although depth was considered necessary, the forward-deployed units were to be the strongest. Counterattacks were to be smaller and more frequent, rather than larger and more ambitious in scope.

This stance was taken due to lack of space to operate in, and the lack of reserve forces for such counterattacks.

Later, mobile defensive tactics were developed that emphasised phases of delay over a limited depth, followed by main defence with strong forces, backed with counterattacks by regrouped units from the delaying force and units withdrawn from less threatened areas.

GROWTH OF THE BUNDESWEHR

NATO forces grew stronger in the 1980s, but the tactical doctrine of holding out at the forward edge of the battle area still dominated West German *Heer* commanders' thinking into the mid-1980s.

The *Bundeswehr* was the largest NATO army in central Europe with a strength of 495,000 regular personnel and about 1,000,000 reserves.

In 1980 the *Heer* introduced a new organisation structure, *Heeresstruktur 4,* designed to allow it to react swiftly to changing developments on the battlefield. Significant changes were made at the brigade and battalion level.

The number of combat battalions in the brigades was raised from three to four and composite tank and armoured infantry battalions were created with both types of company under the one battalion command. In the field platoons were often swapped between companies, so that a *Panzergrenadier Kompanie* (Armoured Infantry Comp-any) would operate with a *Panzer Zug* (Tank Platoon) attached and the *Panzer Kompanie* (Tank Company) would receive a *Panzergrenadier Zug* (Armoured Infantry Platoon).

The army fielded three corps under NATO, one each in the three main army groups. The 1st German Corps was in the Northern Army Group (NORTHAG) with the Dutch, British and Belgians. The 3rd German Corps was south of the Belgians in the Central Army Group (CENTAG) with two US Corps. Finally, the 2nd German Corps was in the Southern Army Group (SOUTHAG) facing Czechoslovakia, with French support. In addition, one German division was allocated to Land Forces Jutland (LANDJUT) defending the Baltic approaches and Denmark alongside the Danish forces.

THE BUNDESWEHR GOES TO WAR

Panzer Brigade 2 HQ, 3 August 1985

Before presenting his final instructions to his staff, Oberst Karl Hauff stepped closer to the map to study the symbols that represented the units of Panzer Brigade 2 and the divisional support elements attached to it. To him, they were more than neat blue markings meticulously posted to the map by his staff. To him, they were men, tanks, infantry fighting vehicles, and self-propelled guns. They were all out there in the pre-dawn darkness waiting. Waiting for other men represented by red symbols to cross a line that had divided his country for forty years. It was inevitable, he sadly concluded, this day would come, a day that would determine, once and for all, the fate of Germany and its people.

Turning, Hauff took a moment to study the faces of men he'd honed into an effective instrument of war. He knew that behind the dispassionate expressions each wore like masks, they entertained the same niggling apprehensions that haunted him. "This is not the time to give into your fears," Hauff concluded as he drew himself up. "We are ready," he declared crisply. "The motto of this division is 'Go! Let's Tackle it!' It is what is expected of us, and what we must do. If no one has any questions, you are dismissed."

There were no questions.

MOBILISATION

With the tension in the Persian Gulf escalating through July and the Americans mobilisation beginning on 28 July, the German Chancellor announced the call up of West German reserves on 29 July, and the full-mobilisation of the *Bundeswehr* on 1 August 1985.

Although negotiations were ongoing at the government level in the hope of a diplomatic solution, the *Bundeswehr* continued its mobilisation, putting into action all the years of preparations and training that had readied it for war. Their Allies in the Dutch government awaited the outcome of the negotiations before mobilising, thereby delaying the deployment of the 1st Netherlands Corps to their positions to the north of the 1st German Corps. This forced the Germans to redeploy forces to cover the Dutch positions as well as their own. *Panzergrenadier Division 6*, the sole German division in LANDJUT, deployed south of its intended positions. The Dutch 1st Armoured Division deployed in the middle of the Dutch sector, while the *Panzer Division 3* stretched northward to meet them. The spread-out positions of the 1st German Corps left them exposed to attack by two Soviet armies, the 2nd Guards Tank Army in the north and the 3rd Shock Army to its south.

West Germany's 2nd and 3rd Corps' mobilisation and deployment went smoother. Units filled out with reservists and took up their defensive positions. The 3rd German Corps took positions to the north of the Americans holding the Fulda Gap and the route to Frankfurt, while the 2nd German Corps' positions straddled the Danube River between Nürnburg and Munich.

THE ATTACK

During the early hours of 4 August 1985 the Soviet 3rd Shock Army crashed into the 1st German Corps. To the north the Soviet 2nd Guards Tank Army thrust through the area held by *Panzergrenadier Division 6* towards Hamburg. They found no Dutch troops, only Germans who had spread out thinly to hold the front. The Soviet armoured thrust pushed on through towards Hamburg and Bremen, hounded at every turn by continuous German counterattacks. The units of the 1st German Corps were too few in number to delay the Soviets for long, even with reservist troops making many units over strength, but their efforts went some way towards slowing the advance and allow the rest of the 1st Netherland Corps to get into action around Bremen and Bremerhaven.

A Soviet airborne landing around Bremen and Bremerhaven attempted to cut off the Dutch and German troops as they withdrew westwards, but vigorous defence by reserve units was able to hold the way open.

A new defence was quickly established along the Weser and Aller Rivers. The 1st German Corps withdrew in contact with the northern flank of the 1st British Corps while swinging their northern flank southwest to maintain contact with the Dutch. After fighting a series of delaying actions and fighting withdrawals, the 1st German Corps eventually pulled back across the Mittelland Kanal (Midland Canal) to establish new defensive positions around Osnabrück.

THE CENTRE

The 3rd German Corps in CENTAG became embroiled in the fighting for the Fulda Gap as the Soviet 8th Guards Army punched through the area. They joined the Americans in defending the position, launching spoiling attacks to slow the Red Army's advance, eventually bringing it to a halt by 12 August.

THE SOUTH

The 2nd German Corps faced the Czechs and supporting Soviets along the Danube River valley as they thrust towards Munich. Further east Soviet forces quickly crushed resistance in neutral Austria and launched a drive through the mountains towards Munich from the south. The Germans and remnants of the Austrian Army fought delaying actions all along the front as they played for time. Meanwhile, the 2nd French Corps had been joined by the 1st French Corps and reinforced the SOUTHAG front, eventually halting the enemy advance west of Munich.

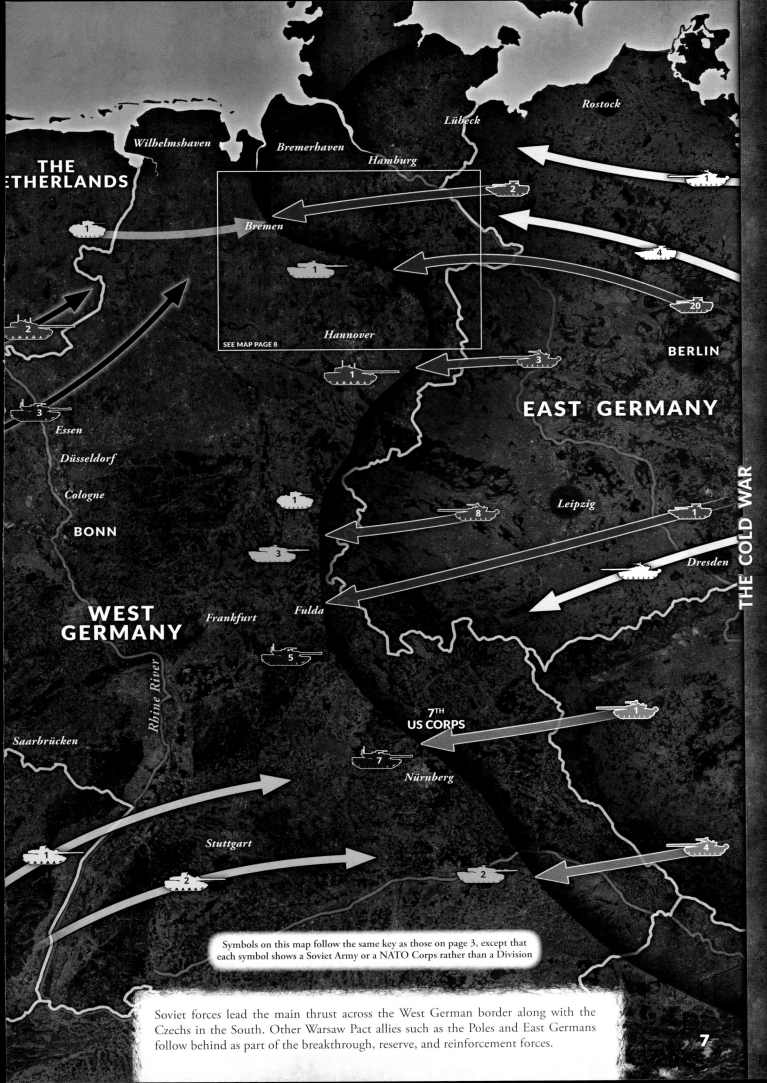

THE NETHERLANDS

Wilhelmshaven

Bremerhaven

Hamburg

Lübeck

Rostock

Bremen

SEE MAP PAGE 8

Hannover

BERLIN

EAST GERMANY

Essen

Düsseldorf

Cologne

Leipzig

BONN

Dresden

WEST GERMANY

Frankfurt

Fulda

Rhine River

Saarbrücken

7TH US CORPS

Nürnberg

Stuttgart

Symbols on this map follow the same key as those on page 3, except that each symbol shows a Soviet Army or a NATO Corps rather than a Division

Soviet forces lead the main thrust across the West German border along with the Czechs in the South. Other Warsaw Pact allies such as the Poles and East Germans follow behind as part of the breakthrough, reserve, and reinforcement forces.

PANZER DIVISION 1

The tensions between NATO and the Warsaw Pact had heightened over July, casting a shadow over *Panzer Bataillon 24's* celebration of the NORTHAG victory in the Canadian Army Trophy tank gunnery competition. As it became clear that things were not going to be resolved through diplomatic channels, *Panzer Division 1* prepared itself for war. When the order came down to mobilise they were ready to take up their positions facing the inner German border east of Hannover and Braunschweig (Brunswick).

The first to mobilise and deploy was *Panzer Brigade 2* from Braunschweig, just 45km (28 miles) from the major border crossing near Helmstadt and less than 40km (25 miles) from the smaller crossing point at Wolfsburg to the northeast. The brigade deployed its battalions covering the likely avenues of Soviet advance between Wolfsburg and Helmstadt. The brigade was joined by the reconnaissance battalion, *Panzeraufklärungs Bataillon 1,* which deployed piquets on the border watching for movement and any attempt by the East Germans to clear their minefields for additional crossing points.

The Division's two other brigades, *Panzergrenadier Brigade 1* and *Panzer*

Brigade 3 deployed in their planned defences east of Hannover. Once *Panzer Brigade 2* had delayed the Soviet onslaught long enough they would retire behind Brigades 1 and 3 to take on the role of reserve and counterattacking force.

THE SOVIETS ATTACK

The mobilisation and deployment had gone like clockwork, but this was followed by several days of nervous waiting. It was in the early hours of 4 August 1985 that the quiet was finally broken. Across the front of *Panzer Brigade 2,* massive artillery and air strikes fell amongst the troops' positions. News followed that *Panzeraufklärungs Bataillon 1* and *Panzer Brigade 2* were under attack and had engaged Soviet forces crossing the frontier.

The Leopard 1 tanks of the reconnaissance troops engaged the various probes across the border, while Leopard 2 tanks and *panzergrenadier* infantry of the brigade engaged elements of several tank columns crossing at Wolfsburg and Helmstadt.

At Wolfsburg the Soviets advanced up the railway line with their BMP scout vehicles. These were easily knocked out by the Leopard 2 tanks of *Panzer Bataillon 21,* but the Soviets soon brought up T-72 main battle tanks in battalion strength, which forced the Germans to withdraw through the town to their next position.

At Helmstadt, the Soviets used the Autobahn to by pass the town and push across the border, following a prolonged artillery barrage. *Panzer Bataillon 24* quickly reacted, counter-

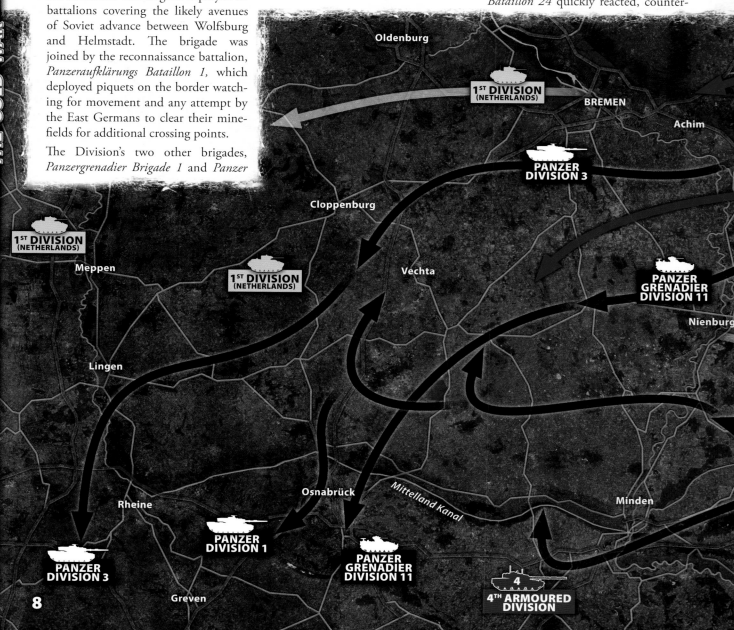

attacking into the flank of the Soviet column. With the German tanks harassing them from the cover of Helmstadt, the Soviets launched an attack on the German battalion's positions, which finally pushed them out of the town. *Panzer Bataillon 24* withdrew northwest following the Autobahn. At Süpplingenburg they left one company, Kampfgruppe Müller, to cover Soviet thrusts directly west from Helmstadt.

Engagements continued like this for the first day, with the battalions and companies of *Panzer Brigade 2* engaging the Soviets, doing just enough to bring them to a halt and then withdrawing to the next ambush position. Two days of dogged delaying actions and local counterattacks forced the Soviets to change their approach. On 6 August they halted their thrusts directly at *Panzer Brigade 2*. Leaving a pinning force, they redirected their thrust northwestwards, bypassing Braunschweig.

NORTHWARD DEFENCE

With the British deployed in their sector south of Hannover, the brigades of *Panzer Division 1* were free to concentrate on the defence north of Hannover. To the division's north, things were not going as well for *Panzergrenadier Division 11*, with only one brigade equipped with Leopard 2 tanks, they were unable to hold back the massive employment of Soviet armour and were forced to withdraw more frequently. With space opening up between the two divisions, *Panzer Brigade 2* were withdrawn behind *Panzergrenadier Brigade 1* and into reserve. The division's front now ran between Celle in the north and Braunschweig in the south, with *Panzergrenadier Division 11* on their northern flank, the British to the south and behind them in Hannover.

COUNTERATTACK

A counterattack was organised to take pressure off *Panzergrenadier Division 11* to the north. The Soviet 47th Guards Tank Division had pushed passed Celle as the panzergrenadiers withdrew, exposing their flank. *Panzer Brigade 2* organised an armoured battlegroup to attack the enemy flank. They quickly brushed aside the Soviet flank guard and hit the rear of the Soviet tank formation before they had time to react. The Leopard 2 main battle tanks proved their worth in a series of running battles, and the lead elements of the Soviet division were soon burning wrecks. *Panzer Brigade 2* cut its way through several tank battalions before Soviet follow on forces forced them to disengage, but not before they had brought the Soviet momentum to a halt. Continuous pressure to the north forced the division to withdraw again to avoid leaving its flank hanging.

Prolonged combat, preceded by massive artillery bombardments every time the Soviets attacked, were wearing the division down. Less than half of their tanks were still running, and then only due to the efforts of recovery and maintenance crews to get the damaged vehicles back into action. Meanwhile, the flood of Soviet armour seemed unabated.

9TH TANK DIVISION

Bispingen

Bad Bevensen

Soltau

Uelzen

10TH GUARDS TANK DIVISION

Walsrode

KAMPFGRUPPE MÜLLER'S BATTLES

1   See pages 12, 13, and 14

2   See page 15

Essel 2

Buchholz

Celle

3

12TH GUARDS TANK DIVISION

Langenhagen

Wolfsburg

PANZER DIVISION 1

HQ

PANZER DIVISION 1
DEPLOYMENT AREA

47TH GUARDS TANK DIVISION

HANNOVER

2

Braunschweig

1

Helmstedt

207TH MOTOR RIFLE DIVISION

Hildesheim

1

4TH ARMOURED DIVISION

THE FRONT SWINGS

By 11 August the Dutch had been pushed back past Hamburg, Bremen, and finally beyond their own borders. In the meantime *Panzer Division 3* had withdrawn through the Dutch to form a new 1st German Corps reserve. To maintain contact with the Dutch, *Panzergrenadier Division 11* withdrew across the Mittelland Kanal (Midland Canal). *Panzer Division 1* screened them as they continued their running battles with troops of the Soviet 3rd Shock Army. With the successful withdrawal of *Panzergrenadier Division 11* completed and in new defensive positions on the high ground north of Onsabrück over-looking the Mittelland Kanal, *Panzer Division 1* began to withdraw across the canal on 12 August. The division formed defensive brigdeheads at a number of key bridges, holding them until both civilians and withdrawing troops had crossed.

Panzer Division 1 withdrew across the Mittelland Kanal and took up defensive positions between Osnabrück and the Dutch border to reorganise.

NATO REINFORCEMENTS

In the meantime the 3rd US Corps had moved up from reserve to join 1st German Corps and the 1st British Corps to prepare for a major counter-offensive northwards towards Bremen and Hamburg.

Under the command of the 3rd US Corps, a multinational force of German, US, British and Belgian units assembled for the attack. *Panzer Division 1* was to deploy on the left of the main US thrust to smash through the forces facing their positions west of Osnabrück, before cutting across the lines of supply and communications of the Soviet 2nd Guards Tank Army and 20th Guards Army. Both they and the relatively fresh *Panzer Division 7* are to protect the flank of the 3rd US Corps, countering any attacks coming from the rear by the Soviets or their Polish and East German allies. The war had reached a turning point.

NATO STRIKES BACK

With much of the momentum exhausted by fierce defence across all sectors, NATO command decides to go on the offensive before further Soviet reinforcements arrive. In NORTHAG an attack, led by the 3rd US Corps, is launched from the British bulge southwest of Hanover towards Wilhelmshaven. Its aim is to cut off the Soviet and Polish forces that had advanced into the Netherlands. Though led by the Americans, the force was made up of units from US, British, Belgian, and German divisions.

Panzer Division 1 and *Panzer Division 7* from the 2nd German Corps quickly turn from defence to attack.

Panzer Division 7 will push north to clear the northern Netherlands of Soviet and Polish forces, while Panzer Division 1 will push along the Dutch border towards Bremerhaven and Hamburg on the left flank of the 3rd US Corps' thrust.

The Germans also play a leading role in the CENTAG counterattack. The 3rd German Corps makes it to the inner German border allowing the 7th US Corps to springboard from their positions and launch towards Leipzig and Berlin in East Germany.

Once these objectives are secured NATO's next objective will be to take the war to the Warsaw Pact and follow-up their success with a drive into East Germany.

THE COLD WAR

KAMPFGRUPPE MÜLLER

Extract from the War Journal of Kompanie 2, Panzer Bataillon 24
4 August 1985

Pursuant to orders from battalion, Kompanie 2 occupied its primary fighting positions east of Süpplingburg, at 0335 hrs Alpha, immediately followed by stand-to. Initial dispositions, from north to south were as follows;

- Panzer Zug 2

- Panzer Zug 3

- Panzergrenadier Zug 2, Kompanie 7, Panzergrenadier Bataillon 22

- Company HQ section

- Panzer Zug I

The first indication hostilities had commenced came promptly at 0400 hrs when Soviet artillery commenced a bombardment of positions occupied by the divisional covering force.

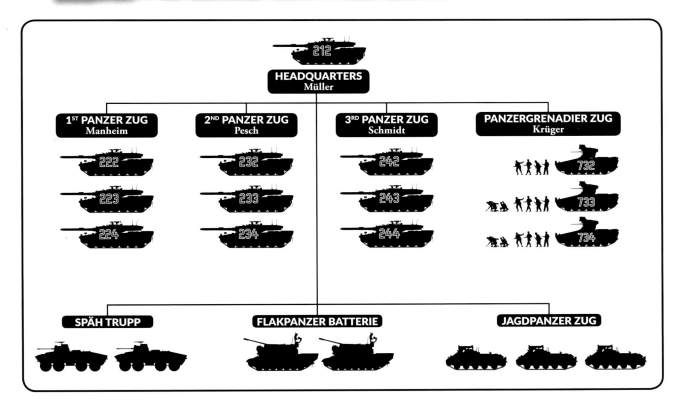

Hauptmann (Captain) Ernst Müller's panzer company was part of *Panzer Bataillon 24, Panzer Brigade 2,* of *Panzer Division 1.* Mobilisation and deployment had been a rush of checking equipment and logistic tasks as the whole brigade prepared to take up their forward positions east of Braunschweig. Under his command he had three *Panzer Züge* (Tank Platoons), and a *Panzergrenadier Zug* (Armoured Infantry Platoon), which had been attached from *Panzergrenadier Bataillon 22* in exchange for his fourth *Panzer Zug.* In addition, he also had attachments of brigade troops in the form of a *Späh Trupp* (scout troop) of two Luchs eight-wheeled armoured cars, and a *Jagdpanzer Zug* (Tank-hunter Platoon) of three Jaguar 1 tank-hunters armed with the powerful HOT anti-tank guided missile, and from the divisional troops, a *Flakpanzer Batterie* (Anti-aircraft Battery) of two Gepard Flakpanzer anti-aircraft tanks.

With his small *Kampfgruppe* (Battlegroup) he was to hold the village of Süpplingenburg on the L644 road leading from the northern suburbs of Helmstadt for as long as possible. To the North was the Autobahn 2 motorway and *Panzer Bataillon 23,* to his south was *Panzergrenadier Bataillon 22.* Forward of his position were the rest of his battalion in Helmstadt. Müller had deployed his platoons along the eastern edge of Süpplingenburg facing the L644. From their positions along the tree lined edge of the village the platoons could observe everything coming in their direction. To further warn of approaching enemy Müller had pushed out his Luchs *Späh Trupp* about 1500m (nearly a mile) further down the L644.

SÜPPLINGENBURG

0500 hours, Sunday 4 August

It was the rumble of artillery hitting Helmstadt, followed by the crack of gun fire in the distance that broke the still of the night in the early hours of 4 August. It wasn't long before the *Späh Trupp* broke radio silence and reported the approach of Soviet panzers down the L644. The advance was led by BMP scout vehicles, followed by T-72 tanks.

The Luchs appeared shortly afterwards and raced into the village. Across the front of the village, *Hauptmann* Müller's men waited patiently for the Soviets to arrive.

As the silhouettes of the approaching tanks could be seen against the predawn light, the Jaguar 1 tank-hunters were first to fire, launching their HOT missiles and destroying three T-72 tanks seconds later. The burning wrecks illuminated the surrounding vehicles and the ten Leopard 2 panzers unleashed their guns on them. The rest of the lead T-72 company was soon ablaze.

The following Soviet tanks halted, before reversing back the way they had come. Müller's boys has done well in their first battle.

PUSHED WEST

1100 hours, Sunday 4 August

Müller realised that his position wouldn't remain unmolested for any length of time. Expecting Soviet artillery to start falling amongst his platoons at any moment, he quickly checked his map for a new position. He moved his *Kampfgruppe* to a tree-lined field southwest of the village, while sending the *Späh Trupp* and the 3rd *Panzer Zug* to watch the northern flank. As anticipated, the artillery fell on Müller's previous position, which was quickly followed by attacks to the north and south of the village.

In the north a flight of two Mi-24 Hind attack helicopters swept over the position of the 3rd *Panzer Zug* firing their anti-tank missiles. The smoke from one burning Leopard 2 tank was soon seen rising above the village. Intense anti-aircraft fire from the company's Gepards ensured the Hinds abandoned another attack run. The helicopter attack was closely followed by a company of T-72 tanks. After a short firefight, *Leutnant* Schmidt, the Leopard platoon commander, decided to withdraw his remaining two Leopard 2 tanks through the village towards the rest of the company. The Luchs withdrew down a side road to loop around the north of the village.

1115 hours

On the southern flank Müller once more found a good concealing position with a clear view of the Soviet advance, about 500m from Süpplingenburg. Müller and his men waited patiently for the Soviet attack to develop. This time the Soviets had deployed line-abreast before advancing, firing their 125mm tank guns as they advanced. They peppered the tree line of Müller's

previous positions with high-explosive rounds.

At 750m Müller gave the order to open fire. A tirade of muzzle blasts sounded along the tree line. Explosions erupted along the Soviet line, followed by several secondary explosions as ammunition stowage cooked out, sending two T-72 turrets flying into the air. However, Müller's position was now exposed, and the Soviet tankers were soon returning fire. One young German tank commander was thrown from his turret when his tank took a hit, and another Leopard was knocked out, killing the driver and wounding the gunner and loader.

With one tank knocked out, and another with a shaken crew, Müller began retiring his battlegroup by platoons. As they retired they knocked out two more T-72s, eventually moving to the town of Königslutter am Elm.

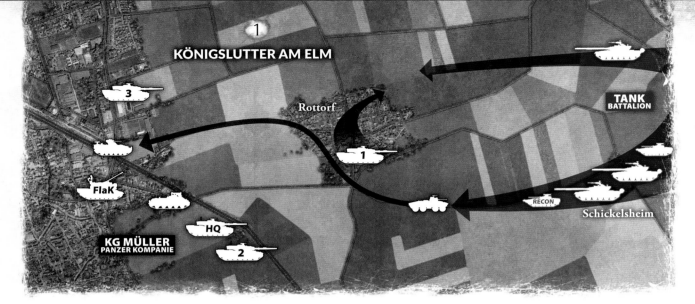

KÖNIGSLUTTER AM ELM

05:00 hours, Monday 5 August

The roar of engines was heard in the small hours of the morning. The *Späh Trupp*, positioned in Schickelsheim, immediately alerted Müller, who had deployed his platoons across the front of Königslutter am Elm, with Manheim's Leopard 2 Panzer Zug in the village of Rottorf, 1000m ahead of the rest of the company.

The two Luchs of the *Späh Trupp* soon appeared racing down the road. About 30 seconds later, three BMP-2s followed more cautiously. T-72 tanks and more BMP-2s emerged from the darkness behind them, deploying to the right of the L644. The BMP-2s fired their 30mm cannons at the rapidly retreating Luchs armoured cars, hammering chunks out of the tarmac before getting the range. A shot struck the trailing Luchs and blew off a wheel just as it swerved into the cover of Rottorf.

As soon as the *Späh* troops had passed, Manheim's platoon, lurking in Rottorf, opened fire. Ignoring the BMP-2 scouts, they trained their guns on T-72 tanks. As the heat of the Soviet tanks' engines glowed green in their thermal imaging sights, the Leopards opened fire and hit three T-72s. The Leopard crews, working with practiced efficiently, quickly sent another three rounds slamming into three more T-72s. The remaining T-72 tanks slewed their turrets towards the village. With rounds blasting the surrounding houses, Manheim pulled back his tanks to the north side of Rottorf.

With the T-72 tanks distracted, the 2nd *Panzer Zug*, under *Leutnant* Pesch,

and the Jaguar 1 tank-hunters began to pick off more of the Soviet tanks.

To the northwest, concealed in the trees surrounding a factory complex on the edge of the town, *Leutnant* Schmidt, with his two remaining Leopard 2 tanks, sighted the Luchs emerging from Rottorf. As he watched them fleeing his way, he noticed some movement to the left of Rottorf. A line of tanks about 1800m to the east. Switching to the platoon net, Schmidt alerted *Feldwebel* Gruber in the platoon's other tank, *"Achtung Panzer! Osten!"* He then contacted Müller with a situation report.

Schmidt's platoon fired on the approaching left flank T-72s, and were joined by Manheim's platoon from Rottorf. The five Leopard 2 tanks poured fire into the Soviet T-72 company. Taking damage, it halted and withdrew northeast, leaving several burning wrecks behind. South of Rottorf, the Soviets also retreated.

LOOK TO THE NORTH

0700 hours, Monday 5 August

At about 0700 hours a cry of *"Achtung panzer! Nordosten"* came over the company net, *Leutnant* Schmidt had spotted movement to the northeast. No sooner had Müller brought his field glasses up to see, when his position was rocked by a series of explosions. Dust and smoke soon engulfed his tank. Müller quickly ducked down and closed his commander's hatch to avoid the artillery. On the radio Schmidt reported a large group of tanks and BMPs about 2.5km (1.5 miles) from his position making west towards the southern edge of Rieseberger Moor. After contacting the battalion headquarters, Müller learnt that they were

heavily engaged by an armoured assault along the autobahn and unable to head off this new Soviet drive.

Leaving the Luchs to watch the east, Müller moved his platoons west along the B1 road to the village of Lauingen, utilising the tree lined railway embankment to conceal their movement. As they arrived in the village the first Soviet vehicles were seen emerging from a gap in the Moor. A hastily issued plan saw the panzergrenadiers and jagdpanzers finding concealed locations along the edge of the village amongst the gardens and the Gepards positioned behind. The Leopards moved to the woods north of the village.

Much to Müller's consternation, the Soviets halted and began deploying into battle formation while his company was still moving into position. They did not react, and once deployed facing Rieseberg, simply stopped. The arrival of a flight of SU-25 Frogfoot strike jets, screaming towards Rieseberg, appeared to be what they were waiting for, and the Soviet tanks began moving north.

The delay had been enough. With his company in position, Müller gave the order, *"Feuer Frei!"*

Across the front of Lauingen a wall of HOT and Milan anti-tank missiles, and 120mm Sabot rounds blasted out to strike the unsuspecting Soviets. Exploding tanks contrasted against the dark background of the forest.

A second line of Soviet vehicles passed through their burning countrymen and turned to face the new threat. Müller's men were ready once again and fired on the new targets. A wave of return fire erupted across the front. On the right a Jaguar 1 took a hit and was consumed by smoke and fire. Other Soviet rounds tore through the trees and buildings at the edge of the village. Another German volley put an end to that.

A third echelon of Soviet tanks had continued heading north. Müller led his nine tanks off in pursuit. As the Soviets approached another wooded area to the north, a number of flashes were seen along the forest edge. It seemed the battalion had been able to redeploy some tanks to the flank. Several T-72 tanks rolled to a halt, billowing smoke as the crews bailed out. Müller's tanks joined the fray, sending more rounds in to the rear of the Soviet formation. More flashes from the forest edge added to the turmoil and more T-72 tanks were left ablaze. The remaining few enemy tanks broke off and turned east and made for the nearby woods.

ATTACK TO THE ALLER

0815 hours, Wednesday 7 August

After a welcome few days in reserve *Kampfgruppe* Müller was in action again. The battalion had been ordered to attack. They were to thrust towards Buchholz and secured the bridges across the Aller River.

Kampfgruppe Müller formed the left flank of the battalion and were to take and hold Essel, a village 1.5km (1 mile) northwest of Buchholz, a crossing point on Aller River. Müller's *Kampfgruppe* was covering the left flank, securing Essel and its bridge.

At 0800 hours, the battlegroup's Luchs reached Essel, the Leopards following behind, while the Jaguars and panzergrenadiers covered the right flank facing east.

As Schmidt's 3rd Panzer Zug entered the Essel, a fusillade of RPG rockets welcomed them. The other two panzer platoons probed around the right of the village. A sudden "woosh" alerted Müller that they had found the Soviets. RPG rounds flew out of a copse of trees to the right of Essel. More followed, exploding against the thick front armour of Manheim's tanks. The Leopards slewed their turrets towards the fire and opened up with their machine-guns.

The Luchs, ignored by the Soviets, raced through the village to the bridge. Their advance was brought to a sudden halt by the appearance of a T-72 tank exiting the bridge. Reporting their discovery, both Luchs quickly reversed back towards Essel.

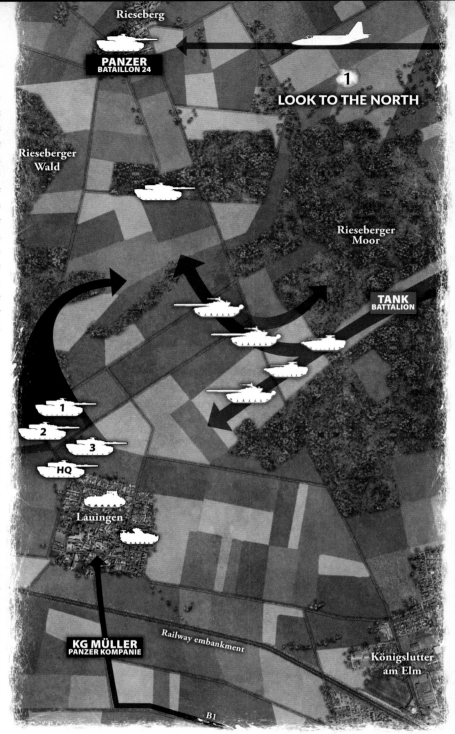

Müller, making a quick appraisal of the situation, ordered *Leutnant* Pesch's panzer platoon past Manheim's platoon and towards the bridge. He then called the panzergrenadier platoon forward to deal with the infantry in the village.

Manheim's platoon pushed through the copse forcing the infantry to scatter, with most of the survivors fleeing in the direction of the bridge.

Müller joined Pesch's platoon as it advanced on the bridge. They pushed through a thicket of trees and shrubs to the north of a side road and were greeted with the sight of a column of T-72 tanks rolling towards them. Pesch's platoon immediately opened fire, and just as they were trained to do, knocked out the leading tank and the trailing tank. This forced the Soviet tanks to begin deploying off the road to the left and right. The Soviets fired as they did so. One of Pesch's tanks took a hit and two of its crew quickly bailed out and retreated into the bushes. Pesch's two remaining tanks made quick work of the T-72 tanks to the right. Müller reversed out of cover to engage the tanks that moved to the left, leaving three more tanks destroyed by the time he was finished.

Meanwhile, the panzergrenadiers had arrived at the village and began clearing it with support from their Marders and Schmidt's tanks, forcing the Soviet infantry northwards towards the river.

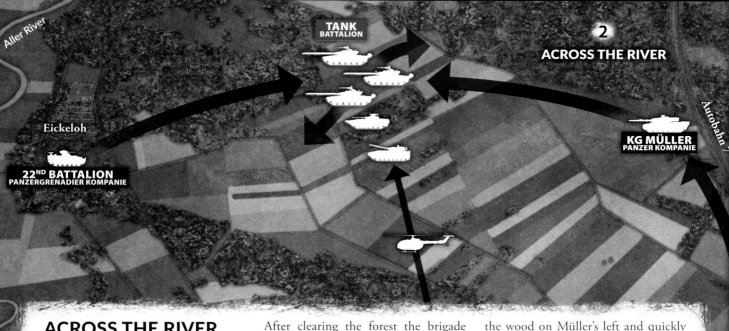

TANK
BATTALION

KG MÜLLER
PANZER KOMPANIE

Eickeloh

22ND BATTALION
PANZERGRENADIER KOMPANIE

Aller River

Autobahn 7

ACROSS THE RIVER

1300 hours, Wednesday 7 August

With the crossings over the Aller secured, the brigade commander decided to push over the river and engage the exposed flank of the Soviets pushing westwards. *Kampfgruppe* Müller, supported by a flight of PAH helicopters, would advance up *Autobahn 7*, with *Panzergrenadier Bataillon 22* deployed on their left to take a series of villages on the north bank of the Aller.

Kampfgruppe Müller advanced from their positions around Essel, across the Aller River and through the forest to the north of the river for about 1000m.

After clearing the forest the brigade scouts reported a large concentration of tanks stopped to northwest about 2km from the Aller River. Müller was ordered to coordinate his attack with a company of panzergrenadiers who were to attack from Eickeloh through the woods to the west. Müller was to attack from the southeast.

As the Kampfgruppe approached the woods screening the positions of the Soviets from the east, lead elements sighted a group of 2S1 Carnations facing Eickeloh firing in the direction of the Panzergrenadier company. Müller contacted the PAH helicopters and they popped above

the wood on Müller's left and quickly dispatched them.

Müller then pushed to the north of the burning Carnations, with the PAHs skipping ahead to a new concealing position. Müller's leading platoon rounded the wood and were faced with a battalion of tanks and a company of infantry parked in several long tree lined fields. The German tanks were quickly spotted, which sent the Soviets into a mad scramble to mount their vehicles. The Leopards began to pick off the stationary T-72s as they desperately tried to swing their guns into action. Retaliation came quickly, a volley of sabot rounds and anti-tank missiles began flying in the Germans' direction, with two Leopards taking hits.

Just as Müller was considering withdrawal, the panzergrenadier battalion to the southwest began to engage. A number of Soviet vehicles were struck in the flank by tank gun rounds and Milan anti-tank missiles, causing further panic and indecision among the Soviet Army ranks. As the noose tightened around the Soviet position a number of vehicles made a break directly south past the right flank of the panzergrenadiers. However, these came under attack from the PAH helicopters who rained HOT missiles into their flanks, while Leopard 2 tanks pressed them from the north and south. The will to fight wavered as the last T-72 was put out of action and the remaining infantry and crews attempted to escape into the woods where they were rounded up by the panzergrenadiers.

In the following days Kampfgruppe Müller would see much more action in the defence of Germany.

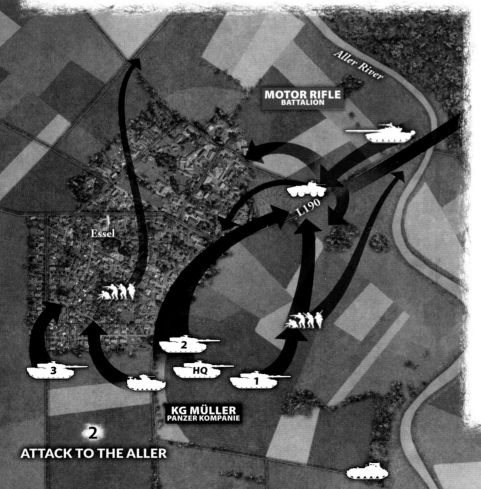

Aller River

MOTOR RIFLE
BATTALION

L190

Essel

2
HQ
3
1

KG MÜLLER
PANZER KOMPANIE

2

ATTACK TO THE ALLER

16

17

PANZER DIVISION 1

Panzer Division 1 (1st Armoured Division) was formed initially in 1956 with the creation of the first division, Grenadier Division 1, for the newly formed *Heer* (Army) of the *Bundeswehr* (Federal Defence Forces). Its first members were mainly drawn from *Grenzschutzkommando Nord* (Border Guard Command North) based in Hannover. In 1959 a new army structure (*Heeresstruktur II*) was introduced and the division became Panzergrenadier Division 1. With the introduction of *Heeresstruktur IV* (Army Structure 4) in 1981 the division changed composition so it contained two Panzer Brigades and one Panzergrenadier Brigade and was re-designated Panzer Division 1.

From its creation, *Panzer Division 1* has been stationed in the area of Hannover and Lower Saxony with the Command Staff headquarters in Hannover. From 1981 its various elements were stationed around Lower Saxony, with Panzergrenadier Brigade 1 in Hildesheim, Panzer Brigade 2 in Braunschweig, and Panzer Brigade 3 in Nienburg.

The divisions close association with the city of Hannover and the region of Lower Saxony led to the division taking on the title of the 'Lower Saxony Division' (*Niedersächsische Division*) in 1983.

The battlefield role of the German Panzer division was as a mobile armoured strike force, but its deployment as part of Germany's strategy of forward defence meant some divisions were deployed eastward as far as possible.

Within the 1st German Corps, Panzer Division 1, along with Panzergrenadier Division 11, would hold the forward positions of the corps' sector. Panzer Brigade 2, in turn, held the forward positions of Panzer Division 1. For this task Panzer Brigade 2 was held at an increased level of preparedness, ready at short notice to absorb any attacks that may come across the inner border with East Germany. For this roll Panzer Brigade 2 was stationed around Braunschweig (Brunswick) near several major border crossing points.

The defence was not intended to be static, but to consist of delaying actions and counterattacks to keep the enemy unsure as to when they had reached the main line of resistance. It was also intended to give the rest of the division and corps time to prepare defences and fully deploy. Later, as the battle developed, the Panzergrenadiers were to be used to hold, delay and pin enemy forces while the armoured forces were used to counter-attack. The highly mobile nature of the German forces meant that they could easily change the direction and location of these attacks, withdraw at short notice, and generally keep the enemy uncertain.

PANZER DIVISION 1

PANZER BRIGADE 2

PANZER BATAILLON 21
PANZER BRIGADE 2

PANZER BATAILLON 21
LEOPARD 2
PANZER KOMPANIE
TG101

PANZERGRENADIER BATAILLON 22
PANZER BRIGADE 2

PANZERGRENADIER BATAILLON 22
MARDER
PANZERGRENADIER
KOMPANIE
TG104

PANZERAUFKLÄRUNGS BATAILLON 1
PANZER DIVISION 1

PANZERAUFKLÄRUNGS BATAILLON 1
PANZERAUFKLÄRUNGS
KOMPANIE
TG110

RAKENTENARTILLERIE
BATAILLON 12

PANZER DIVISION 1
LARS
RAKETENWERFER
BATTERIE
TG120

PANZER DIVISION 1
M113 OP
TG121

FLUGABWEHR
REGIMENT 100

PANZER DIVISION 1
ROLAND
FLARAKPANZER
BATTERIE
TG122

HEERESFLIEGER
REGIMENT 16

PANZER DIVISION 1
PAH
ANTI-TANK
HELICOPTER FLIGHT
TG123

LUFTWAFFE

PANZER DIVISION 1
TORNADO
STRIKE
FLIGHT
TG124

A smile crept across Hauptmann Müller's lips as he watched the lead elements of a column of Soviet tanks emerging from behind a tree line to his front right and deploy. Like an arrow that had been loosed, they headed unerringly for the village field where his company's tanks had been, a field now smothered in bright, angry flashes and smoke. Had he not taken the initiative and moved his tanks from it, Müller had little doubt the enemy's well orchestrated assault would have blown through them without pausing.

"Well, my friends, you are about to be treated to a truly nasty surprise," Müller muttered as he waited a bit longer to demonstrate in a most brutal fashion that Leopard was more than a name someone long ago had thought would be appropriate for a modern killing machine. It was a state of mind, one no different than his tank's namesake. The Leopard was a cunning beast that stalked its prey, patiently biding its time until that one golden opportunity presented itself. Only then did it spring, felling its hapless victim in a wild, violent frenzy of claws and fangs.

When the lead Soviet tanks reached a line on the ground that only existed in Müller's head, he keyed his radio mike. "Achtung Panzer! This is Müller. FIRE!"

With a single, sharp crack that echoed back to another era, the ten Leopards belonging to Müller's company unleashed a devastating volley that turned the Soviet tank battalion's parade ground maneuvering into utter chaos. Like a stunned beast, the commanders of those tanks that were not hit in the first volley traversed their turrets to their left and right, frantically trying to spot where their assaulters were. Some spotted Müller's new position right off. Few of those who did had any opportunity to do anything about it other than slew their main guns around, an act that made it easy for Müller's gunners to decide which enemy tanks to engage next.

For his part, Müller had little need to give any further orders to his company. Just as his commander had given him a mission and the freedom to carry it out, Müller was able to allow his tank commanders to go about their duties. It was, in the mind of the young panzer company commander, exactly what his ancestors had had in mind when they coined the phrase *auftragstaktik* (mission tactics).

Panzer Division 1 was typical of a *Heer* panzer division with two panzer brigades (*Panzer Brigade 2* and *Panzer Brigade 3*) armed with Leopard 2 main battle tanks. Each panzer brigade contained three panzer battalions, a panzergrenadier battalion and a panzer artillery battalion.

Panzer Brigade 2 had two Panzer battalions (23rd and 24th), each consisting of three panzer companies equipped with thirteen Leopard 2 tanks each. The third battalion (21st), was mixed with a Panzergrenadier Kompanie with Marder infantry fighting vehicles and two panzer companies of Leopard 2 tanks. Meanwhile, the Panzergrenadier battalion (22nd) provides flexibility as the brigade's infantry battalion.

The panzer brigade is well-equipped, with its own supporting arms, even before divisional and corps support is called on. Each brigade has its own Panzerjager Kompanie with Jaguar 1 tank-hunters armed with HOT anti-tank missiles, panzergrenadiers, and armoured artillery, as well as signals, supply and engineering troops.

It was common for platoons to be exchanged between battalions and companies to ensure a company had the infantry or armoured support it required to complete its combat mission.

Anti-aircraft assets from the division's anti-aircraft regiment were also allocated to brigades and battalions to provide excellent cover with their Gepard Flakpanzers and Fliegerfaust 1 anti-aircraft missiles.

As the forward brigade of Panzer Division 1, Panzer Brigade 2 would be the first to engage the enemy. Their role was to delay the enemy aggressively, buying time for the rest of the division to deploy and prepare, before withdrawing to reserve to take up the counterattacking role.

PANZER DIVISION 1
LEOPARD 2 PANZERKOMPANIE

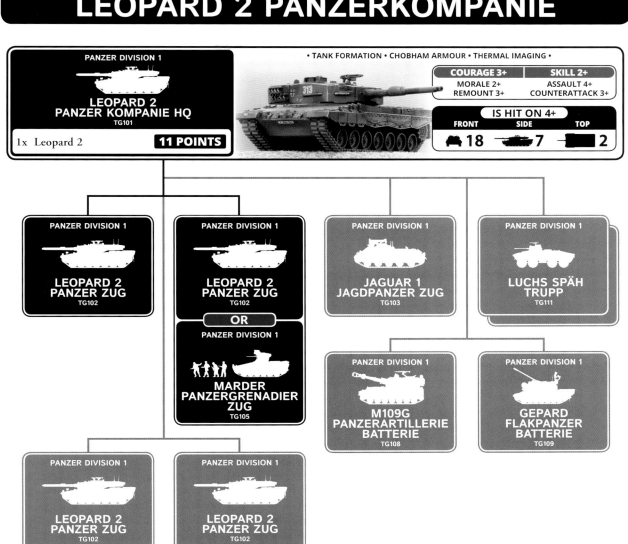

PANZER DIVISION 1
LEOPARD 2 PANZER KOMPANIE HQ
TG101

1x Leopard 2 **11 POINTS**

• TANK FORMATION • CHOBHAM ARMOUR • THERMAL IMAGING •

COURAGE 3+	SKILL 2+
MORALE 2+	ASSAULT 4+
REMOUNT 3+	COUNTERATTACK 3+

IS HIT ON 4+

FRONT	SIDE	TOP
18	7	2

PANZER DIVISION 1
LEOPARD 2 PANZER ZUG
TG102

PANZER DIVISION 1
LEOPARD 2 PANZER ZUG
TG102

OR

PANZER DIVISION 1
MARDER PANZERGRENADIER ZUG
TG105

PANZER DIVISION 1
JAGUAR 1 JAGDPANZER ZUG
TG103

PANZER DIVISION 1
LUCHS SPÄH TRUPP
TG111

PANZER DIVISION 1
M109G PANZERARTILLERIE BATTERIE
TG108

PANZER DIVISION 1
GEPARD FLAKPANZER BATTERIE
TG109

PANZER DIVISION 1
LEOPARD 2 PANZER ZUG
TG102

PANZER DIVISION 1
LEOPARD 2 PANZER ZUG
TG102

WEST GERMAN FORCES

LEOPARD 2 PANZER ZUG

WEST GERMAN FORCES

LEOPARD 2 PANZER ZUG

3x Leopard 2	**33 POINTS**
2x Leopard 2	**22 POINTS**

The Leopard 2 came about from the joint German-US 'Battle Tank 70' program, which was abandoned after costs rose above what the West German government was willing to spend. However, out of the ashes arose a phoenix, the outstanding Leopard 2 main battle tank. The first prototypes developed by Krauss-Maffei were delivered for testing in 1972. The 1973 Yom Kippur War between Israel and Egypt highlighted the importance of armoured protection, and the Leopard 2 developed into a much more heavily armoured vehicle than its predecessor the Leopard 1. Its composite armour, incorporating layers of different material with various protective characteristics,

• TANK UNIT • CHOBHAM ARMOUR • THERMAL IMAGING •

COURAGE 4+	SKILL 3+
MORALE 3+	ASSAULT 4+
REMOUNT 3+	COUNTERATTACK 4+

IS HIT ON 4+		
FRONT	SIDE	TOP
18	7	2

TACTICAL	TERRAIN DASH	CROSS COUNTRY DASH	ROAD DASH	CROSS
14"/35CM	20"/50CM	32"/80CM	32"/80CM	2+

WEAPON	RANGE	ROF HALTED	ROF MOVING	ANTI-TANK	FIRE-POWER	NOTES
120mm L/44 gun	40"/100CM	2	2	22	2+	Advanced Stabiliser, Laser Rangefinder
7.62mm AA MG	16"/40CM	3	3	2	6	
7.62mm MG	16"/40CM	1	1	2	6	

improved its protection against a variety of anti-tank warheads, while allowing it to retain the extraordinary speed of it predecessor.

Initially the prototypes were fitted with 105mm guns, but a new more powerful smooth-bore 120mm gun by Rheinmetall was selected (the same gun that would eventually be fitted to the American's M1 Abrams tank). Combined with a excellent fire-control system, stabilisation, a laser range-finder, and firing Armour-Piercing Fin-Stabilised Discarding Sabot (APFSDS) penetrator rounds, the Leopard 2 has proved itself time and time again the best tank in NATO shooting competitions.

Crew:	4 - commander, gunner, loader, driver
Weight:	55 tonnes
Length:	9.67m (31' 8.7")
Width:	3.7m (12' 1.6")
Height:	3m (9' 10")
Weapons:	Rheinmetall 120mm L/44 Gun 2x MG3 7.62mm MG
Armour:	Chobham - 350 to 620mm RHA equivalent, 520 to 950mm RHA against HEAT
Speed:	72 km/h (45 mph)
Engine:	MB 873 Ka-501 V-12 Twin-turbo diesel engine, 1,500 hp (1,103 kW)
Range:	550 km (340 miles)

M109G PANZERARTILLERIE BATTERIE

M109G PANZERARTILLERIE BATTERIE	
3x M109G	**7 POINTS**

Each Panzer Brigade and Panzergrenadier Brigade was supported by it own *Panzerartillerie Bataillon* (Armoured Artillery Battalion) equipped with M109G *Panzer-haubitze* (armoured howitzer). These were refitted US M109A1 self-propelled guns with a new muzzle brake, improved breech, panoramic telescope and armoured targeting scope.

• TANK UNIT •

COURAGE 4+		SKILL 3+	
MORALE 3+		ASSAULT 5+	
REMOUNT 4+		COUNTERATTACK 5+	

IS HIT ON 4+		
FRONT	SIDE	TOP
2	2	1

TACTICAL	TERRAIN DASH	CROSS COUNTRY DASH	ROAD DASH	CROSS
10"/25CM	16"/40CM	24"/60CM	28"/70CM	3+

WEAPON	RANGE	ROF HALTED	ROF MOVING	ANTI-TANK	FIRE-POWER	NOTES
M126 155mm howitzer	88"/220CM	ARTILLERY		4	2+	*Smoke Bombardment*
or Direct fire	24"/60CM	1	1	12	1+	*Brutal, Slow Firing, Smoke*
7.62mm AA MG	16"/40CM	3	3	2	6	

Crew: 6 - commander, 2x gunner, 2x loader, driver
Weight: 25.5 tonnes
Length: 9.1m (30')
Width: 3.15m (10'4")
Height: 3.25m (10'8")

Armour: 20mm
Weapons: M126 155 mm howitzer
MG3 7.62mm MG
Speed: 56 km/h (35 mph)
Engine: Detroit Diesel 8V71T diesel, 450 hp (335.56 kW)
Range: 350 km (216 miles)

JAGUAR 1 JAGDPANZER ZUG

JAGUAR 1 JAGDPANZER ZUG	
3x Jaguar 1	**6 POINTS**
2x Jaguar 1	**4 POINTS**

The Jaguar 1 is a development of the *Kanonen-jagdpanzer* (Cannon Tank-hunter), a 90mm gun-armed tank-hunter introduced in the 1960s. The first anti-tank missile-armed version was the *Raketenjagdpanzer 1* (rocket tank-hunter) armed with the SS-11 anti-tank missile. 316 of these vehicles were uparmoured and converted to mount the new HOT anti-tank missile system between 1978 and 1983 as the Jaguar 1.

HOT (*Haut subsonique Optiquement Téléguidé Tiré d'un Tube,* or High-subsonic Optical remote-guided, Tube-launched) is a long-range anti-tank missile system. The HOT missile system as fitted the Jaguar 1 was designed to be

• TANK UNIT • INFRA-RED (IR) • FORWARD DEFENCE •

COURAGE 4+		SKILL 3+	
MORALE 3+		ASSAULT 5+	
REMOUNT 4+		COUNTERATTACK 5+	

IS HIT ON 4+		
FRONT	SIDE	TOP
9	4	1

TACTICAL	TERRAIN DASH	CROSS COUNTRY DASH	ROAD DASH	CROSS
10"/25CM	16"/40CM	28"/70CM	32"/80CM	3+

WEAPON	RANGE	ROF HALTED	ROF MOVING	ANTI-TANK	FIRE-POWER	NOTES
HOT missile	8"/20CM - 48"/120CM	1	-	23	3+	*HEAT, Guided.*
7.62mm AA MG	16"/40CM	3	3	2	6	
7.62mm MG	16"/40CM	1	1	2	6	

used under NBC protection and the missile could be retracted into the vehicle for reloading using an automated loading system.

The Jaguar 1 equipped the *Panzerjäger* companies of the Panzer Brigades where their role was to provide long-range anti-tank support to the *Panzer-truppen* (armoured troops).

One – two – three. It had been as easy as that. Three BMP-1s emerged from the village that sat at the foot of the two hills occupied by Oberleutnant Kurtz's platoon, and the three had been neatly dispatched by his own Milan gunners and a pair of Jaguar 1 jagdpanzers supporting them. Only now did he realise he'd been too hasty in giving the order to fire, a mistake he expected he'd soon regret, for the commander of the Soviet motor rifle company to which those three BMPs belonged was, no doubt, rousting his troops out of the surviving BMPs in preparation for a more deliberate dismounted assault. One Kurtz imagined would be supported by artillery. When it came, he told himself this time, to wait for more vehicles to come into view.

That thought had no sooner crossed his mind when a screech he'd only heard in the cinema caused him to drop down into the turret of his Marder. The urge to order his driver to back away from the edge of the tree line and deeper into the forest that had hidden his platoon from observation was rejected out of hand. He needed to stand fast, if for no other reason than to keep the commanders of his other Marders from thinking they'd somehow missed an order to withdraw and begin to displace to their secondary positions. His orders had been clear. He was to hold his position until it was no longer tenable. Just what that meant wasn't so obvious.

"Here they come," Kurtz's gunner announced crisply as he pressed his eye tightly against the rubber cup of his sight and slewed the turret slightly to the left.

Catapulted back to the here and now, without giving what he was doing a second thought, Kurtz popped his head up out of the still open hatch and scanned the open ground to his front, now covered with dismounted Soviet infantry and BMPs.

"Not yet," he muttered. "Not yet."

The front-line German infantry are panzergrenadiers (armoured infantry) mounted in Marder infantry fighting vehicles. Panzergrenadier brigades in a panzer division consist of three panzergrenadier battalions, one panzer battalion and a panzer artillery battalion. Panzer brigades also have one panzergrenadier battalion and one panzergrenadier company in one of its three panzer battalions.

A panzergrenadier battalion consisted of three panzergrenadier companies and a *Panzermörser Kompanie* (armoured mortar company). These heavy 120mm mortars mounted in M113 APCs provided immediate fire support the battalion.

Further support comes from the brigade troops and attached divisional and corps units.

The mobility and versatility of the panzergrenadiers lends them to a variety of combat roles. The speed and protection offered by their Marder armoured fighting vehicles is well-suited for swift changes between mounted and dismounted combat. This enables them to keep pace with their tanks while still being able to clear villages and dense terrain that can't be entered or held by the tanks. This versatility and ability to react quickly enables them to gain and maintain the initiative in fluid battle situations. Key to this success is the combination of fire and movement, while attacking in conjunction with the Leopard main battle tanks.

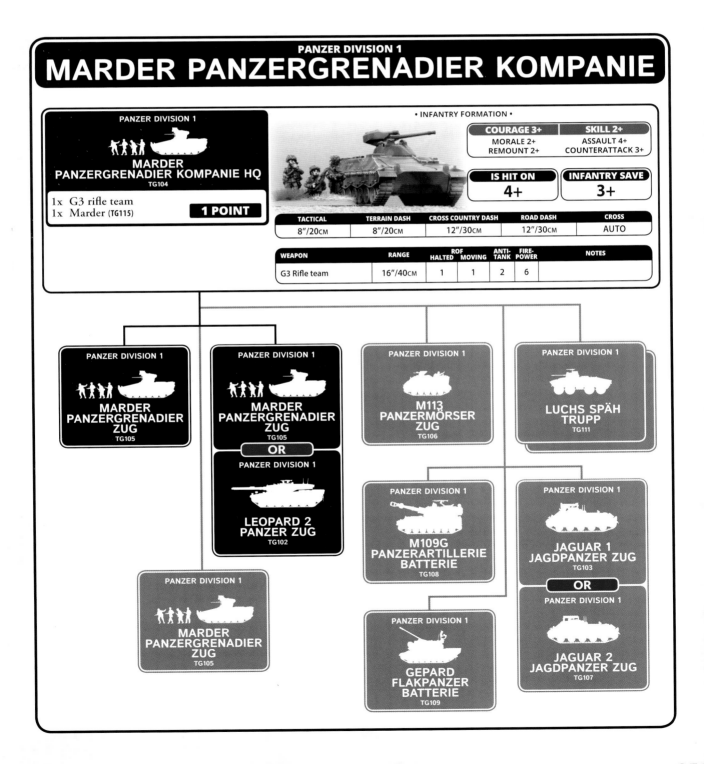

MARDER PANZERGRENADIER ZUG

MARDER PANZERGRENADIER ZUG

3x MG3 team with
Panzerfaust 44 anti-tank rocket
2x Milan missile team
3x Marder (TG115)   **7 POINTS**

2x MG3 team with
Panzerfaust 44 anti-tank rocket
1x Milan missile team
2x Marder (TG115)   **4 POINTS**

MILAN MOUNT: *A Panzergrenadier Zug (TG105) may remove Milan missile teams before the game, mounting a Milan missile on one of the Unit's Marders for each team removed.*

• INFANTRY UNIT • THERMAL IMAGING •

COURAGE 4+		SKILL 3+	
MORALE 3+		ASSAULT 4+	
RALLY 3+		COUNTERATTACK 4+	

IS HIT ON	INFANTRY SAVE
4+	3+

TACTICAL	TERRAIN DASH	CROSS COUNTRY DASH	ROAD DASH	CROSS
8"/20CM	8"/20CM	12"/30CM	12"/30CM	AUTO

WEAPON	RANGE	ROF HALTED	ROF MOVING	ANTI-TANK	FIRE-POWER	NOTES
MG3 team or	16"/40CM	3	2	2	5+	
Panzerfaust 44 anti-tank	12"/30CM	1	1	15	5+	*HEAT, Slow Firing*
Milan missile	8"/20CM - 36"/90CM	1	-	21	3+	*Assault 5, Guided, HEAT*

MARDER TRANSPORT

• TANK ATTACHMENT • THERMAL IMAGING • MILAN MOUNT • PASSENGERS 2 •

COURAGE 4+		SKILL 3+	
MORALE 3+		ASSAULT 4+	
REMOUNT 4+		COUNTERATTACK 4+	

IS HIT ON 4+		
FRONT	SIDE	TOP
3	1	1

TACTICAL	TERRAIN DASH	CROSS COUNTRY DASH	ROAD DASH	CROSS
10"/25CM	20"/50CM	28"/70CM	36"/90CM	3+

WEAPON	RANGE	HALTED	MOVING	ANTI-TANK	FIRE-POWER	NOTES
20mm Rh 202 gun	20"/50CM	3	2	7	5+	*Anti-helicopter*
7.62mm MG	16"/40CM	3	3	2	6	
Optional Milan missile	8"/20CM - 36"/90CM	1	-	21	3+	*HEAT, Guided.*

The modern *Panzergrenadier Zug* (Armoured Infantry Platoon) is a small, but well-trained, motivated, and equipped, unit. They ride to battle in the Marder infantry fighting vehicle. Each Marder carried a dismount of seven men, one armed with a MG3 machine-gun, and the rest with G3 assault rifles. In addition one man also had a *Panzerfaust 44* anti-tank rocket, and another was armed with a 40mm *Granat-pistole* (grenade pistol).

Two of the Marders also had a Milan anti-tank missile launcher. This could be either mounted on the vehicle and fired from it, or dismounted and fired from the ground. The third Marder belonged to the *Zug* commander and carried him and his supporting team, including a medic and forward observer for the artillery.

The West Germans are one of the innovators of the infantry fighting vehicle concept. The Marder was the first such vehicle to see service in NATO from 1971. Named after the *Marder* (in English: Marten), a member of the weasel family, it is armed with a MG3 machine-gun and a 20mm Rh 202 auto-cannon to provide the panzergrenadiers with fire support, and can also mount the powerful Milan anti-tank missile system.

Crew: 3 - commander, gunner, driver + 7 passengers
Weight: 28.2 tonnes
Length: 6.79m (22'3")
Width: 3.24m (10'8")
Height: 2.95m (9'9")
Armour: Welded steel 30mm

Weapons: Rheinmetall 20mm Rh 202 Gun
1x MG3 7.62mm MG
Speed: 75 km/h (47 mph)
Engine: MB 833 Ea-500 V6 turbo diesel engine, 600 hp (447 kW)
Range: 520 km (323 miles)

PANZER DIVISION 1
JAGUAR 2 JAGDPANZER ZUG

JAGUAR 2 JAGDPANZER ZUG	
3x Jaguar 2	**5 POINTS**
2x Jaguar 2	**3 POINTS**

While the *Panzerjäger Kompanien* (Tank-hunter Companies) of the panzer brigades are equipped with the Jaguar 1, armed with HOT missiles, the panzergrenadier brigades have Jaguar 2 tank-hunters armed with the US Improved TOW anti-tank missile. The Jaguar 2 tank-hunters have been converted directly from *Kanonenjagdpanzer* 90mm armed tank-destroyer. These have had the gun removed, more armour added, and the TOW mounting fitted so it could be loaded from a hull top hatch by the vehicle crew.

• TANK UNIT • THERMAL IMAGING • FORWARD DEFENCE •

COURAGE 4+	SKILL 3+
MORALE 3+	ASSAULT 5+
REMOUNT 4+	COUNTERATTACK 5+

IS HIT ON 4+		
FRONT	SIDE	TOP
🛡 9	🛡 4	▬ 0

TACTICAL	TERRAIN DASH	CROSS COUNTRY DASH	ROAD DASH	CROSS
10"/25CM	16"/40CM	28"/70CM	32"/80CM	3+

WEAPON	RANGE	ROF HALTED	ROF MOVING	ANTI-TANK	FIRE-POWER	NOTES
Improved TOW missile	8"/20CM - 48"/120CM	1	-	21	3+	HEAT, Guided.
7.62mm AA MG	16"/40CM	3	3	2	6	

Crew: 4 - commander, gunner, loader, driver
Weight: 25.5 tonnes
Length: 6.61m (21'8")
Width: 3.12m (10'3")
Height: 2.55m (8'4")
Armour: 50mm + applique armour

Weapons: Improved TOW missile
2x MG3 7.62mm MG
Speed: 70 km/h (43 mph)
Engine: MTU MB 837 V8 diesel, 500 hp (368 kW)
Range: 335 km (208 miles)

PANZER DIVISION 1
M113 PANZERMÖRSER ZUG

M113 PANZERMÖRSER ZUG	
6x M113 Panzermörser	**6 POINTS**
3x M113 Panzermörser	**3 POINTS**

The panzergrenadier battalions had their very own artillery in the form of 120mm M120 mortars mounted in modified M113 armoured personnel carriers.

The main advantages of these *Panzermörser* (Armoured Mortar) are there mobility and immediate tactical availability. A company commander can request fire as required. For this reason the mortars are nicknamed *'die kleine Artillerie'* (the little artillery).

• TANK UNIT • AMPHIBIOUS •

COURAGE 4+	SKILL 3+
MORALE 3+	ASSAULT 5+
REMOUNT 4+	COUNTERATTACK 5+

IS HIT ON 4+		
FRONT	SIDE	TOP
🛡 3	🛡 2	▬ 0

TACTICAL	TERRAIN DASH	CROSS COUNTRY DASH	ROAD DASH	CROSS
10"/25CM	16"/40CM	24"/60CM	32"/80CM	3+

WEAPON	RANGE	ROF HALTED	ROF MOVING	ANTI-TANK	FIRE-POWER	NOTES
M120 Mörser mortar	64"/160CM	ARTILLERY		3	3+	Smoke Bombardment
7.62mm AA MG	16"/40CM	3	3	2	6	

Crew: 5 - commander, gunner, 2x loader, driver
Weight: 12.5 tonnes
Length: 5.12m (16'9.5")
Width: 2.69m (8'10")
Height: 2.64m (8'8")
Armour: 38mm Aluminium

Weapons: Rheinmetall/Tampella M120 120mm mortar
1x MG3 7.62mm MG
Speed: 62 km/h (38 mph)
Engine: Detroit Diesel V6, 210 hp (154 kw)
Range: 550 km (340 miles)

PANZERAUFKLÄRUNGS·KOMPANIE

WEST GERMAN FORCES

For Feldwebel Stohl, the speed and agility of his Luchs was its most endearing quality. There are, however, limits, he reminded himself as he clung to the open hatch with one hand and the commander's periscope housing with the other in an effort to keep his balance. "Slow down, damn it, before you run us into a ditch Heinie" he yelled out to his driver over the intercom.

With a child-like glee, the driver continued to barrel down the narrow forest trail. "No need to worry about that. I told you, these are my woods. My friend and I used to play in them all the time. In a minute we'll be able to see his house. It's just beyond the next rise."

"Did you ever think Ivan might be there was well?" Stohl snapped.

This less than subtle reminder that they were at war had its effect. With a smartness derived from hours of maneuvering about the battalion's local training area, the driver eased back on the accelerator and brought the eight wheeled armoured car to a speed more appropriate to their tactical situation. It was hard for him to appreciate that this wasn't a peacetime exercise, that they were now at war. The people they were sneaking up on weren't another gang of boys he and his friend often mixed it up with, or soldiers belonging to another NATO army playing at war. They were Russians, Red Army soldiers who, for reasons he couldn't quite grasp, had invaded his country. This next fight, one fought in fields, forests and streets he thought of as his own was one he had trained for, but wasn't quite ready for.

These untimely musings were interrupted by the sound of his commander yelling out commands. "GUNNER! BMP, twelve o'clock. Fire! Franz, back up, back up."

Lifting his gaze from the trail to his immediate front, the driver was stunned to see a Soviet BMP sitting astride the same trail he was on. Even more alarming was the sight of its gun aimed directly at him. He choked back the urge to call out to the rear driver, admonishing him to go faster. All he could do was hope Franz was able to navigate his way back and out of harms way as briskly as he had driven them into it.

The *Panzeraufklärungs Bataillon*, or armoured reconnaissance battalion, of a panzer division provides early warning of the direction and strength of enemy attacks. Their main task is reconnaissance in the area of operations of the parent division.

On the attack, they advance far ahead of the main body locating the enemy positions, defences and intentions, allowing the commander to prepare their attacks as they advance.

In defence, they often operate with reconnaissance by force operations, engaging the enemy to provoke a battle with no intention to fully engage. By observing the reactions of the enemy they can draw conclusions about their numerical strength, equipment, training, competence, and even morale depending on the circumstances. These actions also delay the enemy, leaving them unsure if they have reached the mainline of resistance or not.

A *Panzeraufklärungs Bataillon* is made up of two heavy companies equipped with Leopard 1 tanks, a mixed company with Leopard 1 tanks and Luchs 8-wheeled armoured cars, and one company of infantry mounted in Fuchs 6-wheeled armoured transports. Often these different elements are allocated out to companies as required for the task at hand.

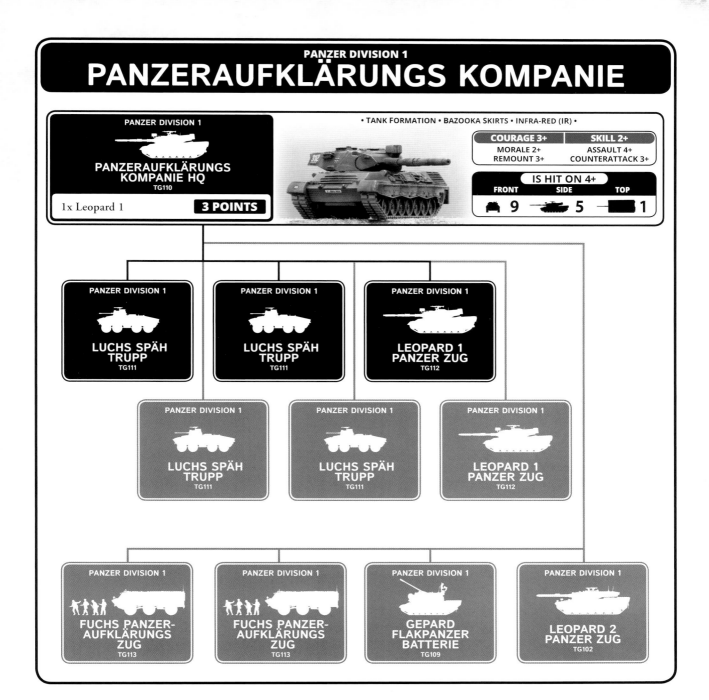

PANZER DIVISION 1
PANZERAUFKLÄRUNGS KOMPANIE

PANZER DIVISION 1
PANZERAUFKLÄRUNGS KOMPANIE HQ
TG110

1x Leopard 1   **3 POINTS**

• TANK FORMATION • BAZOOKA SKIRTS • INFRA-RED (IR) •

COURAGE 3+	SKILL 2+
MORALE 2+	ASSAULT 4+
REMOUNT 3+	COUNTERATTACK 3+

IS HIT ON 4+

FRONT	SIDE	TOP
9	5	1

PANZER DIVISION 1
LUCHS SPÄH TRUPP
TG111

PANZER DIVISION 1
LUCHS SPÄH TRUPP
TG111

PANZER DIVISION 1
LEOPARD 1 PANZER ZUG
TG112

PANZER DIVISION 1
LUCHS SPÄH TRUPP
TG111

PANZER DIVISION 1
LUCHS SPÄH TRUPP
TG111

PANZER DIVISION 1
LEOPARD 1 PANZER ZUG
TG112

PANZER DIVISION 1
FUCHS PANZER-AUFKLÄRUNGS ZUG
TG113

PANZER DIVISION 1
FUCHS PANZER-AUFKLÄRUNGS ZUG
TG113

PANZER DIVISION 1
GEPARD FLAKPANZER BATTERIE
TG109

PANZER DIVISION 1
LEOPARD 2 PANZER ZUG
TG102

LUCHS SPÄH TRUPP

• TANK UNIT • AMPHIBIOUS • SPEARHEAD • SCOUT • THERMAL IMAGING •

LUCHS SPÄH TRUPP	
2x Luchs	**1 POINTS**

COURAGE 4+	SKILL 3+
MORALE 3+	ASSAULT 5+
REMOUNT 4+	COUNTERATTACK 6

IS HIT ON 4+		
FRONT	SIDE	TOP
🛡 2	🛡 2	▭ 0

The *Aufklärungs* troops at the very front of the division's vanguard are the *Späh Truppen* (reconnaissance patrols) equipped with the 8-wheeled Luchs armoured car. The Luchs is fast on road, but still has excellent cross-country performance. It is a very quiet vehicle allowing its crew to advance on enemy positions undetected. If they are spotted, the Luchs can reverse at full-speed with the driver switching to a rear facing driving position. It is amphibious and is armed with a rapid-fire 20mm auto-cannon.

TACTICAL	TERRAIN DASH	CROSS COUNTRY DASH	ROAD DASH	CROSS
10"/25CM	12"/30CM	20"/50CM	40"/100CM	4+

WEAPON	RANGE	ROF HALTED	ROF MOVING	ANTI-TANK	FIRE-POWER	NOTES
20mm Rh 202 gun	20"/50CM	3	2	7	5+	
7.62mm AA MG	16"/40CM	3	3	2	6	

LEOPARD 1 PANZER ZUG

• TANK UNIT • BAZOOKA SKIRTS • INFRA-RED (IR) •

LEOPARD 1 PANZER ZUG	
3x Leopard 1	**9 POINTS**
2x Leopard 1	**6 POINTS**

COURAGE 4+	SKILL 3+
MORALE 3+	ASSAULT 4+
REMOUNT 3+	COUNTERATTACK 4+

IS HIT ON 4+		
FRONT	SIDE	TOP
🛡 9	🛡 5	▭ 1

Even though the powerful Leopard 2 main battle tank is now in service throughout the panzer brigades, the Leopard 1 tank has not been retired. One of its roles is now as part of the divisional *Panzeraufklärungs* battalions in the *schwere Panzeraufklärungs Kompanien* (heavy armoured reconnaissance companies) and *gemischte Panzeraufklärungs Kompanie* (mixed armoured reconnaissance company). Though lightly armoured, the Leopard 1 tank is fast and well-armed, with 105mm L7 gun that is more than capable of dealing with any scouting vehicles of Warsaw Pact.

TACTICAL	TERRAIN DASH	CROSS COUNTRY DASH	ROAD DASH	CROSS
10"/25CM	16"/40CM	28"/70CM	32"/80CM	2+

WEAPON	RANGE	ROF HALTED	ROF MOVING	ANTI-TANK	FIRE-POWER	NOTES
105mm L7 gun	40"/100CM	2	2	19	2+	*Laser Rangefinder, Smoke, Stabiliser*
7.62mm AA MG	16"/40CM	3	3	2	6	
7.62mm MG	16"/40CM	1	1	2	6	

Crew: 4 - commander, gunner, loader, driver
Weight: 42.2 tonnes
Length: 9.54m (31' 3.5")
Width: 3.37m (11' 0.5")
Height: 2.7m (8' 10")
Armour: steel 19-21.7mm and 10-70 mm RHA

Weapons: 105mm Royal Ordnance L7A3 L/52 rifled Gun
2x MG3 7.62mm MG
Speed: 65 km/h (46 mph)
Engine: MTU MB 838 CaM 500, 10-cylinder, multi-fuel engine, 819 hp (610 kW)
Range: 600 km (373 miles)

WEST GERMAN FORCES

FUCHS PANZERAUFKLÄRUNGS ZUG

FUCHS PANZERAUFKLÄRUNGS ZUG

3x MG3 team with
   Panzerfaust 44 anti-tank rocket
1x Milan missile team
3x Fuchs (TG114)   **4 POINTS**

2x MG3 team with
   Panzerfaust 44 anti-tank rocket
1x Milan missile team
2x Fuchs (TG114)   **3 POINTS**

MILAN MOUNT: *A Panzeraufklärungs Zug (TG113) may remove Milan missile teams before the game, mounting a Milan missile on one of the Unit's Fuchs for each team removed.*

The infantry element of the armoured reconnaissance battalion is provided by the 5th company. These are organised in a similar fashion to the panzergrenadiers, but only have the one Milan anti-tank missile launcher in each *Zug*. The rest of the men are armed with the same mix of MG3 machine-guns, G3 assault rifles, and Panzerfaust 44 anti-tank rockets as the panzergrenadiers. They are mounted in three Fuchs 6-wheeled *transport-panzer*.

The *Fuchs* (Fox) *Transport-panzer* (abbreviated to *TPz*) is a 6-wheeled, fully amphibious, armoured personnel carrier designed for a variety roles including troop transport, engineer transport, bomb disposal, NBC (Nuclear, Biological and Chemical) reconnaissance and electronic warfare. It can carry up to eight passengers and has an MG3 machine-gun on an anti-aircraft mount. It can also mount a Milan anti-tank missile launcher if mobile firepower is needed. Like the Luchs, it is fast on roads, good cross-country, and is very quiet.

• INFANTRY UNIT • THERMAL IMAGING •

COURAGE 4+	SKILL 3+
MORALE 3+	ASSAULT 3+
RALLY 3+	COUNTERATTACK 4+

IS HIT ON	INFANTRY SAVE
4+	**3+**

TACTICAL	TERRAIN DASH	CROSS COUNTRY DASH	ROAD DASH	CROSS
8"/20CM	8"/20CM	12"/30CM	12"/30CM	AUTO

WEAPON	RANGE	ROF HALTED	ROF MOVING	ANTI-TANK	FIRE-POWER	NOTES
MG3 team or	16"/40CM	3	2	2	5+	
Panzerfaust 44 anti-tank	12"/30CM	1	1	15	5+	*HEAT, Slow Firing*
Milan missile	8"/20CM - 36"/90CM	1	-	21	3+	*Assault 5, Guided, HEAT*

FUCHS TRANSPORT

• TANK ATTACHMENT • AMPHIBIOUS • THERMAL IMAGING • MILAN MOUNT • PASSENGERS 2 •

COURAGE 4+	SKILL 3+
MORALE 3+	ASSAULT 4+
REMOUNT 4+	COUNTERATTACK 4+

IS HIT ON 4+		
FRONT	SIDE	TOP
2	2	0

TACTICAL	TERRAIN DASH	CROSS COUNTRY DASH	ROAD DASH	CROSS
10"/25CM	12"/30CM	20"/50CM	44"/110CM	4+

WEAPON	RANGE	ROF HALTED	ROF MOVING	ANTI-TANK	FIRE-POWER	NOTES
7.62mm AA MG	16"/40CM	3	3	2	6	
Optional Milan missile	8"/20CM - 36"/90CM	1	-	21	3+	*HEAT, Guided.*

Crew: 2 - commander, driver
      + 8 passengers
Weight: 18.3 tonnes
Length: 7.33m (24' 1")
Width: 2.98m (9' 9")
Height: 2.37m (7' 9")

Weapons: MG3 7.62mm MG
Armour: Steel 25mm
Speed: 105 km/h (65 mph)
Engine: Mercedes-Benz Model OM 402A
        V-8 diesel, 320 hp (238 kW)
Range: 800 km (500 miles)

GEPARD FLAKPANZER BATTERIE

• TANK UNIT • INFRA-RED (IR) •

GEPARD FLAKPANZER BATTERIE	
6x Gepard	**15 POINTS**
4x Gepard	**10 POINTS**
2x Gepard	**5 POINTS**

If a force contains a Flakpanzer Batterie, it may also take a Fliegerfaust Gruppe (TG116).

COURAGE 4+	SKILL 3+
MORALE 3+	ASSAULT 5+
REMOUNT 4+	COUNTERATTACK 5+

IS HIT ON 4+

FRONT	SIDE	TOP
3	2	1

TACTICAL	TERRAIN DASH	CROSS COUNTRY DASH	ROAD DASH	CROSS
10"/25CM	16"/40CM	28"/70CM	32"/80CM	2+

WEAPON	RANGE	ROF HALTED	ROF MOVING	ANTI-TANK	FIRE-POWER	NOTES
Twin 35mm L/90 gun	28"/70CM	5	4	11	4+	*Dedicated AA, Radar*

The *Flugabwehrkanonenpanzer* Gepard (Anti-aircraft Cannon Tank, Cheetah), or *Flakpanzer* Gepard for short, is the main anti-aircraft vehicle of the panzer divisions. It is fitted with a sophisticated anti-aircraft radar system for locating and tracking its targets. The Gepard is based on the hull of the Leopard 1 tank, with a large turret mounting a pair of 35mm Oerlikon autocannons and its tracking and search radar dishes.

With a rate-of-fire of 550 rounds per minute for each gun, the Gepard does nasty things to Soviet aircraft. Gepard and Roland anti-aircraft units had multiple crews for 24-hour operations. When not manning their vehicles, these extra crewmen operated *Fliegerfaust 1* (Red-Eye) man-portable anti-aircraft missile systems.

FLIEGERFAUST GRUPPE

• INFANTRY ATTACHMENT •

FLIEGERFAUST GRUPPE	
6x Redeye team	**6 POINTS**
4x Redeye team	**4 POINTS**
2x Redeye team	**2 POINTS**

If your force contains a Gepard Flakpanzer Batterie (TG109) or Roland FlaRakPanzer Batterie (TG122), you may take one Fliegerfaust Gruppe for each Gepard Flakpanzer Batterie (TG109) and one for each Roland FlaRakPanzer Batterie (TG122).

The number of Redeye teams in the Fliegerfaust Gruppe must not exceed the number of Gepard and Roland tanks in your Flakpanzer Batterie and FlaRakPanzer Batterie.

COURAGE 4+	SKILL 3+
MORALE 3+	ASSAULT 4+
RALLY 3+	COUNTERATTACK 4+

IS HIT ON	INFANTRY SAVE
4+	**3+**

TACTICAL	TERRAIN DASH	CROSS COUNTRY DASH	ROAD DASH	CROSS
8"/20CM	8"/20CM	12"/30CM	12"/30CM	AUTO

WEAPON	RANGE	ROF HALTED	ROF MOVING	ANTI-TANK	FIRE-POWER	NOTES
Redeye team	48"/120CM	3	-	-	5+	*Guided AA.*

By accompanying the Gepards and Rolands the *Fliegerfaust 1* teams could take advantage of other anti-aircraft system's long-range detection capacity to give an early warning of approaching enemy aircraft.

PANZER DIVISION 1
PAH ANTI-TANK HELICOPTER FLIGHT

PAH ANTI-TANK HELICOPTER FLIGHT	
4x PAH	**16 POINTS**
2x PAH	**8 POINTS**

The Bölkow Bo-105P was selected as the German PAH anti-tank helicopter (*Panzer-abwehr-hubschrauber*) due to its outstanding manoeuvrability. It is armed with six wire-guided HOT anti-tank missiles, three mounted on each side.

Flying below the tree line, it can sneak up to a firing position unseen, then unleash a deadly attack to smash a Soviet spearhead.

• HELICOPTER AIRCRAFT UNIT • HUNTER-KILLER •

COURAGE 4+	SKILL 3+
MORALE 3+	

IS HIT ON	AIRCRAFT SAVE
4+	**5+**

TACTICAL	TERRAIN DASH	CROSS COUNTRY DASH	ROAD DASH	CROSS
UNLIMITED				AUTO

WEAPON	RANGE	ROF HALTED	ROF MOVING	ANTI-TANK	FIRE-POWER	NOTES
HOT missile	8"/20CM - 48"/120CM	1	-	23	3+	HEAT, Guided.

Hide and Seek

The idea of hiding a 2,500 kg helicopter armed with six HOT missiles was, on the face of it, ludicrous. At the moment, Leutnant Karl Leitz wasn't laughing as his pilot made ready to scurry from behind the hedge they were currently using for concealment to a cluster of trees just off to the left. From there he hoped he would have a clear line of sight into the flank of the column of T-72s they'd been stalking. If not, they'd need to find another spot that would not only keep Ivan's tanks from spotting them until they'd engaged, but

afforded them a chance to break contact and withdraw before the pair of ZSUs mixed in with the tanks were able to bring their guns to bear.

As his pilot prepared to sprint their PAH to the cluster of trees he'd been eyeing, every muscle in his body became taunt in a manner that reminded him of the days when he'd run track for his gymnasium's team.

It was as if he was once again crouching low with his feet pressed against the starter's blocks, plotting out in his mind every step he'd take when the time to spring forward came.

"Here we go," he muttered, more to himself than his pilot as his pilot prepared to break cover. With that, they banked to the left and made straight for their next hide position, keeping one eye on the cluster of trees and the other on the radar warning receiver.

Only when they were set and his pilot had managed to orient the aircraft to where they expected the Soviets would be did their PAH helicopter slowly rise up to treetop level.

PANZER DIVISION 1
LARS RAKETENWERFER BATTERIE

LARS RAKETENWERFER BATTERIE	
4x LARS	**6 POINTS**
2x LARS	**3 POINTS**

OPTION
- Arm all LARS with Minelets for +1 point for the batterie.

LARS (*Leichte Artillerie-raketen-system*, light artillery rocket system) is a self-propelled multiple rocket launcher used by the division's *Raketenartillerie Bataillon* (rocket artillery battalion). The LARS mounts two launcher pods with 18 tubes each. A single LARS launcher is able to fire 36 spin-stabilized 110mm rockets in 18 seconds.

• UNARMOURED TANK UNIT •

COURAGE 4+	SKILL 3+
MORALE 3+	ASSAULT -
REMOUNT 4+	COUNTERATTACK -

IS HIT ON	TANK SAVE
4+	**5+**

TACTICAL	TERRAIN DASH	CROSS COUNTRY DASH	ROAD DASH	CROSS
8"/20CM	8"/20CM	14"/35CM	36"/90CM	5+

WEAPON	RANGE	ROF HALTED	ROF MOVING	ANTI-TANK	FIRE-POWER	NOTES
110mm LARS rocket	80"/200CM	SALVO		3	4+	Smoke Bombardment
7.62mm AA MG	16"/40CM	3	3	2	6	

PANZER DIVISION 1
ROLAND FLARAKPANZER BATTERIE

ROLAND FLARAKPANZER BATTERIE	
6x Roland 2	**9 POINTS**
4x Roland 2	**6 POINTS**
2x Roland 2	**3 POINTS**

If a force contains a Roland FlaRakpanzer Batterie, it may also take a Fliegerfaust Zug (TG116).

The Roland 2 *Flugabwehrraketenpanzer* (abbreviated to *FlaRakPanzer*, or Anti-aircraft Rocket Tank) is a sophisticated mobile short-range surface-to-air missile (SAM) system. The Roland anti-aircraft missile was a joint development between the French and Germans. The Roland 2 is the all-weather German variant and is mounted on the hull of the Marder infantry fighting vehicle.

• TANK UNIT • INFRA-RED (IR) •

COURAGE 4+	SKILL 3+
MORALE 3+	ASSAULT -
REMOUNT 4+	COUNTERATTACK -

IS HIT ON 4+		
FRONT	SIDE	TOP
3	1	1

TACTICAL	TERRAIN DASH	CROSS COUNTRY DASH	ROAD DASH	CROSS
10"/25CM	20"/50CM	28"/70CM	36"/90CM	3+

WEAPON	RANGE	ROF HALTED	ROF MOVING	ANTI-TANK	FIRE-POWER	NOTES
Roland 2 AA missile	56"/140CM	3	-	-	4+	Guided AA

The paired missile launchers can automatically reload in less than 30 seconds from four-round rotary magazines mounted in the hull sides.

The Roland 2 is designed to engage aircraft flying at speeds up to Mach 1.3 at altitudes up to 5,500 meters (18,000 feet). It has a maximum range of 6,300 meters (20,500 feet).

M113 OP

M113 OP	
1x M113 OP	**1 POINT**

You must field:
- *a Panzermörser Zug (TG106), or*
- *a Panzerartillerie Batterie (TG108), or*
- *a Raketenwerfer Batterie (TU120)*

before you may field a M113 OP.

• TANK UNIT • INFRA-RED (IR) • OBSERVER •

COURAGE 4+	SKILL 3+
MORALE 3+	ASSAULT 5+
REMOUNT 4+	COUNTERATTACK 5+

	IS HIT ON 4+	
FRONT	**SIDE**	**TOP**
3	2	1

TACTICAL	TERRAIN DASH	CROSS COUNTRY DASH	ROAD DASH	CROSS
10"/25cm	16"/40cm	24"/60cm	32"/80cm	3+

WEAPON	RANGE	ROF HALTED	ROF MOVING	ANTI-TANK	FIRE-POWER	NOTES
7.62mm AA MG	16"/40cm	3	3	2	6	

The *Beobachtungspanzer Artillerie M113A2GE* (artillery observation tank) was a specialist version of the American M113 armoured personnel carrier. It was fitted with the PERI D11 twin periscope, which included a laser range finder. Sophisticated navigational, data processing, and transmission equipment aided its artillery observation duties.

TORNADO STRIKE FLIGHT

TORNADO STRIKE FLIGHT	
4x Tornado	**8 POINTS**
2x Tornado	**4 POINTS**

The Tornado strike-aircraft was developed as a joint project between Germany, Britain, and Italy.

The main role of the Tornado is as an Interdictor Strike (IDS) aircraft. The Tornado has a variable sweep-wing system. The pilot can change the sweep of the wings to change the aerodynamics of the aircraft. With the wings swept back drag was reduced during critical high-speed low-level dashes towards enemy positions. With the wings swept forward the Tornado takes on the characteristics of slower flight, allowing it to land and take-off on short runways. Low level flight was further enhanced by an innovative automatic terrain-following system.

• STRIKE AIRCRAFT UNIT •

COURAGE 4+	SKILL 3+
MORALE 3+	

IS HIT ON	AIRCRAFT SAVE
4+	**5+**

TACTICAL	TERRAIN DASH	CROSS COUNTRY DASH	ROAD DASH	CROSS
UNLIMITED				AUTO

WEAPON	RANGE	ROF HALTED	ROF MOVING	ANTI-TANK	FIRE-POWER	NOTES
MW-1 submunition dispenser with KB44 bomblet	6"/15cm	SALVO		8	3+	
Mauser BK-27 auto-cannon	8"/20cm	-	3	7	5+	*Anti-helicopter.*

The Tornado is armed with two internally mounted 27mm Mauser BK-27 auto-cannons and two AIM-9 Sidewinder missiles for self-defence. It can carry a variety of conventional bombs, as well as the MW-1 submunition dispenser that drops a variety of munitions, including the KB44 anti-tank bomblet.

WEST GERMAN FORCES

SPECIAL RULES

Serzhant Sergei Bolotenko crept up to the trees lining the road where three the German Leopard tanks sat, their tank commanders engaged in discussion. Bolotenko had no idea what they were discussing, but it didn't matter to him. He had his trusty RPG-7 on hand and he was going to score himself a kill. He'd been told by the Leytenant that the Leopard tank was designed by speed, so wasn't very heavily armoured. He also had a clear view of the rearmost tanks side armour. This was a certainty.

Bolotenko took aim and fired. A "Fuh-ssshhhh" and the rocket was on its way. There was an explosion and a cloud of dust and debris enveloped the Leopard tank.

A smile lit up Bolotenko's face as he admired his handiwork. As the dust cleared he was greeted with the sight of the tank's turret turning to face him.

His blood ran cold as he realised his anti-tank rocket had had no effect.

The *Bundeswehr* has a number of features. These are reflected in the following special rules.

BAZOOKA SKIRTS

The Germans are familiar with the effectiveness of infantry hand-held anti-tank weapons like the original Panzerfaust and Bazooka. The Germans have fitted their modern battle tanks with 'bazooka skirts', spaced armour to protect them from light, hand-held anti-tank weapons.

> Teams with Bazooka Skirts have a Side armour rating of 10 against HEAT weapons.

FORWARD DEFENCE

With the German doctrine of forward defence it is important to have your anti-tank weapons where they can cause the most damage. While most of the panzers are in reserve waiting to counterattack, the Jaguar jagdpanzers are in the front line ready to wreak havoc on the advancing enemy tanks.

> Jaguar 1 or Jaguar 2 Jagdpanzer Zugs can be placed on table in missions with Deep Reserves in addition to the normal limit of one Unit with Front Armour greater than 4.

SCENARIOS

Hauptfeldwebel Braun pondered the possibilities of the next few days as he moved along the positions of his panzergrenadier company. Well, not exactly his, as Hauptmann Knust was in command, but his in the sense that they were all his boys. He'd raised them up from raw recruits. Now they were to face their first test in battle and he was confident they would do well.

It was a clear evening and all was quiet. Braun stopped where a section of the panzergrenadiers had dung-in near the edge of the wood, their positions concealed with foliage. "Are your ready boys?" he inquired.

"Yes Hauptfeldwebel!" they replied in unison.

"You better be when Ivan comes down that road," he indicated to the east with a nod of his head. He patted the Milan operator on the head, "remember Michael, make every shot count."

He then disappeared back into the wood to continue his rounds.

As well as playing the missions in the Team Yankee rulebook, you can also play scenarios inspired by your imagination, your favourite WWIII fiction, or even historical battles put into a WWIII context.

The following scenarios are based on the actions of *Kampfgruppe* Müller and the rest of *Panzer Brigade 2*.

The first scenario, At the Forward Edge of Battle, pits a defending Panzergrenadier Kompanie against the first waves of the Soviet armoured spearhead as they attempt to steam-roll into West Germany. As the German commander, see if you can delay the Soviets long enough using a phased withdrawal, defending one line of objectives before withdrawing to the next line, slowing the Soviet advance. You may like to also try this scenario with an equivalent points of a Panzer Kompanie and see how *Kampfgruppe* Müller would have got on. The challenge for the Soviet player is to push hard and seize the objectives as fast as possible.

The second scenario, Delaying Attack, sees a German force once more buying time, but this time in a more aggressive manner. As a panzer commander you must push forward, utilising the Spearhead rule (see page 71 of the Team Yankee rulebook) of the Luchs Späh Trupp, to deny the Soviets the objectives, once more playing for time and slowing the Red

Army's advance. As a Soviet commander, you'll need to push on to the objective and beyond to clear the way for your advance westwards.

The last scenario, Flanking Attack, is based on *Kampfgruppe* Müller's attack over the Aller River and pits a two-pronged enveloping attack against an over-extended Soviet tank battalion. Be wary, a well organised and lucky player may surprise you and their troops could be more alert than you expect. The Soviet player has to quickly organise his defence against this surprise attack, holding one attack off, while defeating the other in detail using your superior numbers.

You can also play the scenarios in order, using the Consequences and Campaign sections to carry forward the results from one game to another. You can swap sides and play through the campaign to compare your forces and your approaches.

There is also no reason why you can't play all the scenarios with different forces. You can even try different terrain arrangements, as terrain can often make all the difference to how a game plays.

Most importantly of all, have fun and feel free to modify the scenarios anyway you see fit.

Gefreiter Michael Rörig was startled awake by the noise of an explosion and a shower of dirt. He adjusted his helmet and peered over the lip of his foxhole. Further explosions were erupting all around the company's positions. Keeping low, but watchful, he waited as the artillery barrage died down leaving a dusty haze in the early morning light.

He heard them before he saw them. The roar of engines approaching from the east. Rörig grabbed his Milan missile system, attached the missile, and aimed down the road running from the east past his company's positions in the wood. Soldat Schreiber was next to him ready with another missile.

"T-72!" Schreiber announced.

"I see it." The first T-72 emerged through the haze along the road at about 1000 metres. Rörig lined up the tank through the Milan's sights and fired the missile. Keeping the Milan sighted on the T-72 he watch as the silvery trails of wire spooled out behind the missile as it rocketed towards the target. A burst of light, followed a short delay as the crack of the missile hitting home arrived at Rörig and Schreiber's position.

"Got him!" exclaimed Schreiber.

Several more T-72 tanks came into view. Rörig had no time to enjoy his victory, "Reload!"

The 1st German Corps manned its forward positions near the inner German border in the sector between Bad Bodenteich and Schöningen. The Germans knew the Soviets would come in hard, but to allow their allies in NATO time to mobilise, German battalions deployed companies forward to hold and delay the initial Soviet attacks.

Your *Panzergrenadier Kompanie* is in forward positions and must hold up the Soviet advance until the next position is prepared. Once the attack is slowed, your panzergrenadiers will withdraw to the next defensive position.

SPECIAL RULES

- Ambush (Page 100 of Team Yankee)
- Timed Objectives (see below)
- Delayed Objectives (see below)

TIMED OBJECTIVES

Timed Objectives can only be captured before a certain turn. If they are captured before this time is up the Attacker has won the game. After the time limit is up the Timed Objectives are removed from the table and can no longer be captured as their importance to the defenders has ended.

The Timed Objectives are removed at the beginning of the German Turn 3.

DELAYED OBJECTIVES

Delayed Objectives can only be captured after a certain turn. These are placed on the table during Setting Up, but do not become live until the turn indicated by the scenario. The attacker cannot capture a Delayed Objective until it becomes live.

The Delayed Objectives become live at the beginning of the Soviet Turn 4.

SETTING UP

Lay out the terrain on a 6' x 4' (180cm x 120cm) table as shown on the map on the following page.

Place two Timed Objectives on the spots marked .

Place two Delayed Objective on the spots marked Ⓨ.

DEPLOYMENT

The German player holds one Unit in Ambush. They then place the remainder of their forces on the table in the forward deployment area within 12"/30cm of the table centre line in their own table half. The German infantry teams may start the game in Foxholes (see pages 35, 48, and 54 of the Team Yankee rulebook).

The Soviet player then places all their Units within 6"/15cm of their table edge.

STARTING THE GAME

The Soviet Player is the Attacker and has the first turn.

WINNING THE GAME

The Soviet wins the game if they start Turn 2 or 3 Holding one of the Timed Objectives, or start any turn from Turn 4 onwards Holding one of the Delayed Objectives.

Otherwise the German player wins at the start of their eighth turn after checking Formation Morale.

CONSEQUENCES

If the German player wins they have done enough to allow their comrades to take up a new defensive position. If the Soviet player wins, the Germans will be surprised by the speed of the advance as they prepare their counterattack.

WHAT HAPPENED

The panzergrenadiers were able to delay the Soviet forces and then withdraw, inflicting casualties on the attackers and keeping them guessing as to the exact composition and location of the main 1st German Corps' line of resistance.

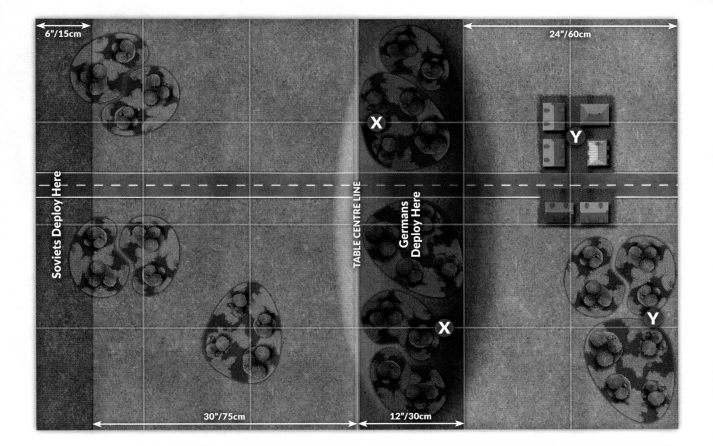

FORCES

PANZERGRENADIER KOMPANIE

Panzergrenadier Kompanie HQ
   1x G3 rifle team
   1x Marder

Marder Panzergrenadier Zug
   3x MG3 team with Panzerfaust 44 anti-tank rocket
   2x Milan missile team
   3x Marder

Marder Panzergrenadier Zug
   2x MG3 team with Panzerfaust 44 anti-tank rocket
   1x Milan missile team
   2x Marder

Jaguar 2 Jagdpanzer Zug
   2x Jaguar 2

Leopard 2 Panzer Zug
   3x Leopard 2

Gepard Flakpanzer Batterie
   2x Gepard

PAH Anti-tank Helicopter Flight
   2x PAH

ALTERNATIVE FORCE: **62 POINTS**

T-72 TANK BATTALION

T-72 Tank Battalion HQ
   1x T-72

T-72 Tank Company
   6x T-72

T-72 Tank Company
   5x T-72

BMP-2 Motor Rifle Company
   7x AK-74 team with RPG-18 anti-tank
   6x RPG-7 anti-tank team
   2x PKM LMG team
   9x BMP-2

BMP-2 Recon Platoon
   2x BMP-2

Mi-24 Hind Assault Helicopter Company
   2x Mi-24 Hind

ALTERNATIVE FORCE: **80 POINTS**

"Yes Sir, we'll get right on it!" finished Hauptmann Hahn. He ended his radio transmission with the battalion commander, switched to the company net and called his platoon commanders together for meeting.

A few minutes later his subordinates gathered around the kitchen table of a local farmhouse.

"Right, battalion wants us to advance to these crossroads," Hahn stabs his finger into the map laid out on the table indicating a road junction about two kilometres from their current position. "Then we are to hold the Soviet advance as long as possible. We are buying time for new defensive positions to be established."

Hahn stepped away from the table and wandered away to gaze out a window. "I want you to be smart, utilise the terrain, don't take unnecessary risks," he paused and turned back towards his men, "but make them pay dearly for those crossroads!"

Returning to the map, Hahn then outlines his plan of attack.

With the Soviets aggressively pushing through the initial defensive positions of the 1st German Corps, the divisional commander organises a local counterattack with a Panzer Kompanie to further delay the Soviet progress. They advance towards the Soviet axis of attack and engage their leading elements in a running battle.

SETTING UP

Lay out the terrain on a 6' x 4' (180cm x 120cm) table as shown on the map on the following page.

Place two Objectives on the spots marked .

DEPLOYMENT

Starting with the German, both players alternate placing Units in their Deployment areas up to 24"/60cm from their corners as shown on the map.

STARTING THE GAME

The German player is the Attacker and has the first turn.

WINNING THE GAME

The Soviet player wins the game if they start any turn from Turn Two Holding any of the Objectives.

The German player wins at the start of any turn from Turn Six with no Soviet teams within 16"/40cm of either Objective.

CAMPAIGN

If the Soviet player won At the Forward Edge of Battle, the German must play Delaying Attack without the Luchs Späh Trupp, therefore losing the ability to use the Spearhead rule (see page 71 of Team Yankee).

If the German player won At the Forward Edge of Battle, they can nominate their Leopard 2 Panzer Kompanie HQ to count as a Spearhead Unit, reflecting the time bought by the forward troops to prepare this attack.

CONSEQUENCES

If the Germans win, they have successfully delayed the Soviet advance and the division's other brigades have deployed across their sector, *Panzer Brigade 2* can safely go into reserve.

If the Soviets win the Germans are pressed for time and are forced to conduct a fighting withdrawal all the way back to the positions of *Panzergrenadier Brigade 1*. *Panzer Brigade 2* will not have the time to rest and re-group.

WHAT HAPPENED

The attack had the effect of slowing the Soviet drive, forcing them to reconsider their direction of attack and buying time for the Germans to withdraw and prepare a new position.

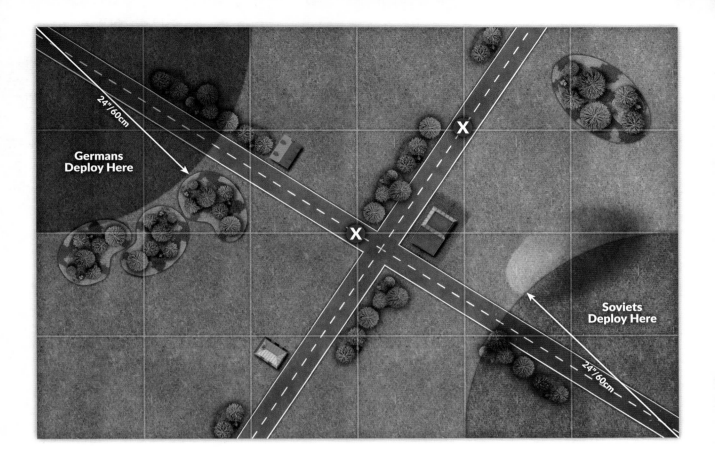

FORCES

PANZER KOMPANIE

Leopard 2 Panzer Kompanie HQ
1x Leopard 2

Leopard 2 Panzer Zug
3x Leopard 2

Leopard 2 Panzer Zug
3x Leopard 2

Luchs Späh Trupp
2x Luchs

Marder Panzergrenadier Zug
3x MG3 team with Panzerfaust 44 anti-tank rocket
2x Milan missile team
3x Marder

Gepard Flakpanzer Batterie
2x Gepard

PAH Anti-tank Helicopter Flight
2x PAH

ALTERNATIVE FORCE: **98 POINTS**

TANK BATTALION

T-72 Tank Battalion HQ
1x T-72

T-72 Tank Company
6x T-72

T-72 Tank Company
6x T-72

T-72 Tank Company
4x T-72

BMP-1 Motor Rifle Company
7x AK-74 team with RPG-18 anti-tank
6x RPG-7 anti-tank team
2x PKM LMG team
9x BMP-1

ZSU-23-4 Shilka AA Platoon
4x ZSU-23-4 Shilka

MI-24 Hind Assault Helicopter Company
2x MI-24 Hind

ALTERNATIVE FORCE: **99 POINTS**

As Müller's panzer kompanie advanced north from Essel, he received a radio call from the Luchs Späh Trupp advancing ahead of them along Autobahn 7. They had discovered signs that a Soviet armoured formation had recently crossed the Autobahn and headed west towards the Aller River.

Müller's Leopard 2 tank pulled up alongside Leutnant Schmidt's tank. "It seems we are definitely behind them," Müller yells over his idling engine, "head north until you can see where the Autobahn has been crossed."

A few minutes later Schmidt came across an area of crushed bushes and churned up muddy verge. It is clear a variety of tracked vehicles has passed through, their trails can be seen cutting through the fields heading westwards.

Müller quickly deployed his company into battle formation in the fields facing west. They begin to roll quietly towards what they hope is the rear of a Soviet unit.

The Soviets have broken through elements of *Panzergrenadier Division 11* and have pushed beyond the town of Celle on your division's flank, threatening to widen a gap between the two front line divisions of the 1ˢᵗ German Corps. Your Panzer Kompanie is to take part in a large brigade counter-attack into the flank of the Soviet drive towards the Aller River. Your brigade is advancing along the northbound Autobahn 7 motorway when scouts alert you to a Soviet armoured battalion to the west between you, on Autobahn 7, and the Aller River.

SPECIAL RULES

- Immediate Reserves (see page 101 of the Team Yankee rulebook)

SETTING UP

Lay out the terrain on a 6' x 4' (180cm x 120cm) table as shown on the map on the following page.

Place two Objectives on the spots marked .

DEPLOYMENT

The Soviet then places all of their units in their deployment area up to 24"/60cm from the side table edge and up to 36"/90cm from the top table edge as marked on the map.

The German player holds the Panzergrenadier Kompanie in Immediate Reserves to arrive from bottom left edge as indicated on the map. The units of the Panzer Kompanie are placed in their deployment area up to 24"/60cm from the side table edge and up to 24"/60cm from the top table edge as marked on the map on the following page.

STARTING THE GAME

The German player is the Attacker and has the first turn.

All Soviet units begin the game Pinned Down and Bailed Out, except for the 2S1 Carnation SP Howitzer Battery, which begins the game in good order.

WINNING THE GAME

The German player wins if they start a turn Holding one of the Objectives.

The Soviet player wins if they start any turn on or after their sixth turn with no German tanks or infantry within 16"/40cm of either Objective.

TERRAIN

Some of the fields are surrounded by irrigation ditches. These are quite narrow and are easily crossed by tracked vehicles. You can model the ditches as streams or brooks and use the terrain rules for a Brook on page 33 of Team Yankee.

CAMPAIGN

If the Soviets won Delaying Attack, the German force doesn't replace its losses, remove one Leopard 2 tank from the first Leopard 2 Panzer Zug that starts on table, and one Leopard 2 tank from the Leopard 2 Panzer Zug in reserve.

If the Germans won, they gain a third Leopard 2 Panzer Zug with two Leopard 2 tanks to their forces that start on table.

CONSEQUENCES

If the Germans win they have smashed the momentum of the Soviet drive, and allowed *Panzergrenadier Division 11* to withdraw and set up strong defences along the Mittelland Kanal.

If the Soviets win, they have halted the German flank attack and are able to continue their drive over the Aller River and smash the retreating *Panzergrenadier Division 11* opening the way to the Rhine.

WHAT HAPPENED

Panzer Brigade 2 cut its way into the rear of a Soviet Tank Division, putting several battalions out of action, but was forced to withdraw when its own flanks came under threat by the Soviets following forces.

SCENARIOS

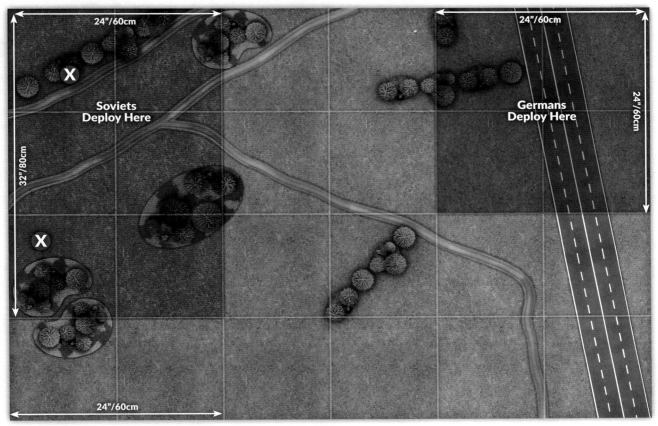

German Reserves Arrive Here

FORCES

PANZER KOMPANIE

Leopard 2 Panzer Kompanie HQ
1x Leopard 2

Leopard 2 Panzer Zug
3x Leopard 2

Leopard 2 Panzer Zug
3x Leopard 2

PAH Anti-tank Helicopter Flight
2x PAH

IMMEDIATE RESERVES

Marder Panzergrenadier Zug
3x MG3 team with Panzerfaust 44 anti-tank rocket
2x Milan missile team
3x Marder

Leopard 2 Panzer Zug
2x Leopard 2

ALTERNATIVE FORCE: 114 POINTS
AT LEAST 28 POINTS MUST START IN IMMEDIATE RESERVES

TANK BATTALION

T-72 Tank Battalion HQ
1x T-72

T-72 Tank Company
7x T-72

T-72 Tank Company
6x T-72

T-72 Tank Company
6x T-72

BMP-1 Motor Rifle Company
7x AK-74 team with RPG-18 anti-tank
6x RPG-7 anti-tank team
2x PKM LMG team
9x BMP-1

ZSU-23-4 Shilka AA Platoon
2x ZSU-23-4 Shilka

2S1 Carnation SP Howitzer Battery
3x 2S1 Carnation

BMP-1 OP Observation Post
1x BMP-1 OP

ALTERNATIVE FORCE: 113 POINTS

PAINTING WEST GERMANS

GERMAN ARMOUR - OLIVE DRAB

LEOPARD 2
NATO CAMO

M109
GELBOLIV

From the 1950's, all of the vehicles in the Bundeswehr were painted in overall *Gelboliv* (Yellow Olive). They started transitioning to three colour Nato camouflage in the early 80s, but there were still examples of overall *Gelboliv* as late as 1989.

To paint West German vehicles in plain *Gelboliv*, simply follow the guide for Painting US vehicles in *Colours Of War* using Cobra Drab as the base colour.

In the 1980's there was no stardardised vehicle numbering system for the West German army, and it was up to commanders how their vehicles were identified.

Kampfgruppe Müller's vehicles (see page 11) are marked with a modified WWII system.

BO-105

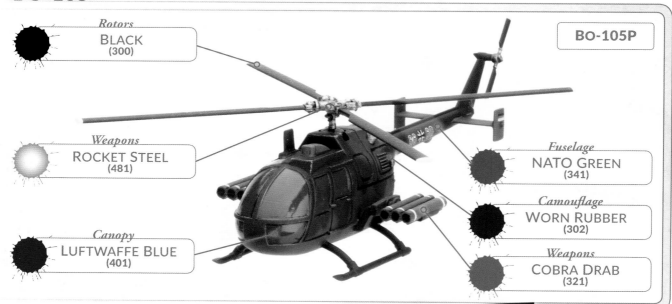

BO-105P

Rotors
BLACK
(300)

Weapons
ROCKET STEEL
(481)

Canopy
LUFTWAFFE BLUE
(401)

Fuselage
NATO GREEN
(341)

Camouflage
WORN RUBBER
(302)

Weapons
COBRA DRAB
(321)

This painting guide uses the *Colours Of War* painting system.

The *Colours of War* book is a detailed and comprehensive guide to painting miniatures that shows you, step-by-step, everything you need to know to field beautifully-painted miniatures in your *Team Yankee* games. While *Colours of War* focuses on the Second World War miniatures of *Flames Of War*, the techniques work just the same for *Team Yankee*.

Visit the *Team Yankee* website: www.Team-Yankee.com for more information.

COLOURS OF WAR
THE ESSENTIAL GUIDE TO PAINTING
FLAMES OF WAR MINIATURES

TEAM YANKEE
WORLD WAR III
MINIATURES GAME

GERMAN PAINT SET

GERMAN ARMOUR - 3 COLOUR NATO CAMOUFLAGE

COLOUR PALETTE

NATO GREEN
(341)

WORN RUBBER
(302)

WOODLAND BROWN
(383)

DRY DUST
(364)

BATTLEFIELD BROWN
(324)

ORDNANCE SHADE
(492)

All West German vehicles were painted to a template, so each vehicle of a particular type will look similar. You can find a useful set of camouflage templates at **www.Team-Yankee.com**

West German vehicle camouflage is usually soft-edged as it is applied by an airbrush. You can replicate this by either using an airbrush or following the soft edge camouflage guide on page 36 of *Colours Of War*.

Alternatively, because of the scale of the models, you could pant the camouflage hard-edge since the 'feather' on the camouflage colours is narrower at 15mm/1:100 scale.

NATO GREEN *Large Brush*

BASECOAT *your tank with NATO Green. Two thin coats are preferable to one thick coat. Alternatively you can use a NATO Green spray can for your undercoat.*

WORN RUBBER *Large Brush*

PAINT *Patches of Worn Rubber in accordance with the paint templates from www.Team-Yankee.com*

WOODLAND BROWN *Large Brush*

PAINT *Patches of Woodland Brown following the paint templates.*

DRY DUST *Large Drybrush*

DRYBRUSH *the tank with Dry Dust, concentrating on edges, raised details, and upper surfaces to add highlights.*

BATTLEFIELD BROWN *Large Brush*

BASECOAT *your tracks with Battlefield Brown. Keep the tracks separate to make them easier to paint. Remember that the top of the track will be hidden by the track guards.*

WORN RUBBER *Small Brush*

WASH *the tracks with Ordnance Shade, then pick out the track pads with Worn Rubber.*

DRY DUST *Small Drybrush*

DRYBRUSH *the lower areas of the tank, concentrating on the flat surfaces, to give the effect of heavy dry dust.*

Adding decals before drybrushing the Dry Dust will help give it the 'painted-on' look

ORDNANCE SHADE *Small Brush*

TARGET WASH *the details with Ordnance Shade to add definition to the vehicle. You may find it easier to apply your target wash if you give the vehicle a coat of gloss varnish first.*

Be sure to visit **WWW.TEAM-YANKEE.COM** for more in-depth painting articles and videos.

GERMAN INFANTRY

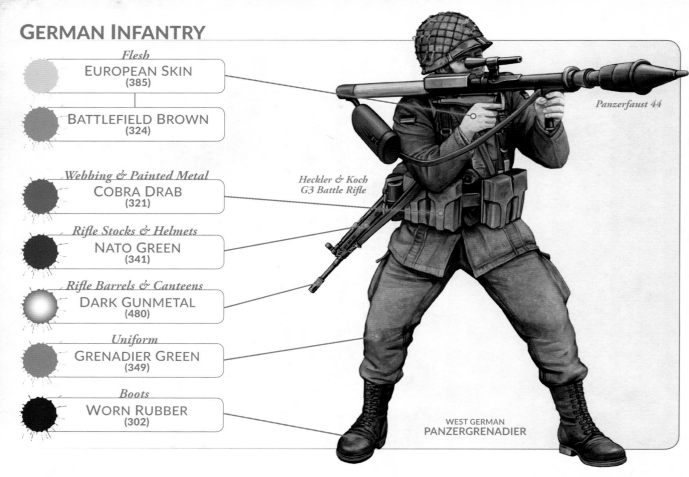

Flesh
EUROPEAN SKIN
(385)

BATTLEFIELD BROWN
(324)

Webbing & Painted Metal
COBRA DRAB
(321)

Rifle Stocks & Helmets
NATO GREEN
(341)

Rifle Barrels & Canteens
DARK GUNMETAL
(480)

Uniform
GRENADIER GREEN
(349)

Boots
WORN RUBBER
(302)

Panzerfaust 44

Heckler & Koch G3 Battle Rifle

WEST GERMAN
PANZERGRENADIER

BASING GERMAN INFANTRY

All *Team Yankee* infantry are supplied with appropriate bases. Assemble your infantry teams by gluing the figures into the holes on a base of the right size. Super glue works well for this.

There are usually several figures with each type of weapon, so you can create variety in your squads. It doesn't matter which figure you put in each team, as long as the mix of weapons is right. Visit the product spotlight on the *Team Yankee* website: www.Team-Yankee.com for a more detailed guide.

Apply a thin coat of plaster filler to the base to give it a bit of texture and fill any gaps between the figures and the holes. Paint your bases Battlefield Brown or a similar earthy colour.

You can then enhance your bases with static grass, flock, and clump foliage.

Colours Of War has a complete basing guide for more information and lots of clever ideas.

Milan anti-tank missile team

Base a Milan anti-tank missile team on a small base.

Formation Commander G3 rifle team

Base the Commander on a small base with a radio operator and rifleman.

MG3 team with Panzerfaust 44 anti-tank rocket

Base a MG3 team on a medium base. Teams combine a machine-gunner armed with an MG3 light machine-gun, riflemen armed with G3 rifles and Panzerfaust 44 anti-tank weapons, and a grenadier armed with an G3 rifle and 40mm Granatpistole (grenade launcher).

Unit Leaders replace the MG3 and grenadier with an officer and radio operator. Some players like to mark their Unit Leaders with a small piece of terrain on the base or a dot of paint on the back of the stand for easy identification.

Redeye team

Base a Redeye missile team on a large base with three Redeye missiles and three rifle-armed assistants.

GERMAN UNIFORMS & WEBBING EQUIPMENT

COLOUR PALETTE

GRENADIER GREEN
(349)

COBRA DRAB
(321)

ORDNANCE SHADE
(493)

WORN CANVAS
(306)

COMRADE KHAKI
(326)

The uniform of Bundeswehr soldiers is a plain olive-green colour.

Try adding a bit of Worn Canvas to the basecoat for some of the soldiers to represent older sun faded uniforms.

GRENADIER GREEN — *Large Brush*

BASECOAT *the uniform Grenadier Green, using two thin coats if necessary to achieve an even coverage.*

COBRA DRAB — *Medium Brush*

BASECOAT *all webbing equipment with Cobra Drab.*

ORDNANCE SHADE — *Large Brush*

WASH *the figure liberally with Ordnance Shade to add depth to the uniform.*

GRENADIER GREEN COBRA DRAB — *Medium Brush*

TIDY UP *uniform and webbing with Grenadier Green and Cobra Drab, leaving shadows in the recessed areas.*

COMRADE KHAKI — *Medium Brush*

DRYBRUSH *the webbing areas with Comrade Khaki.*

75% GRENADIER GREEN 25% WORN CANVAS — *Small Brush*

ACTUAL SIZE

HIGHLIGHT *raised areas of the uniform for a brighter, higher-contrast look.*

GERMAN INSIGNIA

COLOUR PALETTE

CAVALRY YELLOW
(361)

ARTILLERY RED
(380)

BLACK
(300)

CAVALRY YELLOW — *Small Brush*

PAINT *a small square of Cavalry Yellow.* **TIP:** *Underpaint with European Skin for a bright, rich yellow.*

ARTILLERY RED BLACK — *Small Brush*

LAYER *thin lines on Artillery Red and Black over the Cavalry Yellow basecoat.*

GRENADIER GREEN — *Small Brush*

ACTUAL SIZE

TIDY UP *the the edges of the insignia with Grenadier Green.*

SKIN

COLOUR PALETTE

BATTLEFIELD BROWN
(324)

SKIN SHADE
(491)

EUROPEAN SKIN
(385)

BATTLEFIELD BROWN — *Medium Brush*

BASECOAT *the face and hands with Battlefield Brown, in two thin coats.*

SKIN SHADE — *Medium Brush*

WASH *liberally with Skin Shade to create shading and definition.*

50% BATTLEFIELD BROWN 50% EUROPEAN SKIN — *Small Brush*

ACTUAL SIZE

HIGHLIGHT *the most prominent details, like fingertips and the tip of the nose.*

MÜLLER'S WAR

Extract from the War Journal of No. 2 Company, Panzer Battalion 24.

04:00 hrs, 4 August 1985

Luchs belonging to Panzer Aufkarlung I deployed to the company's front, reported contact with a Soviet tank battalion's advanced guard consisting of a BMP-2 recce platoon. After stripping the tank battalion of its advanced guard and forcing it to deploy, the Späh trupp withdrew along L644 through the company's positions.

Müller felt a chill run down his spine as the lead Soviet tank company began to emerge from the predawn gloom like ethereal specters that were so much a part of Germanic folklore. The T-72s, however, were not the product of a storyteller's fertile imagination. They were real, as real as his own tank. That thought caused him to look to his right and along the thin tree line his company and the Jaguar 1 jagdpanzers were deployed along. The jagdpanzers would open the engagement when the first of the Soviet tanks reached the designated trigger point. Only when the first of their HOT missiles hit home would Müller's Leopard 2 tanks join in.

Two quick flashes, followed by pops and whoosh of the rocket engine of a pair of HOT missiles lit up the predawn darkness. Twisting about, Müller watched. Despite having been waiting for the jagdpanzers to fire, the event nonetheless caught him off guard, causing him to forget to issue a fire command to his gunner. Not that he needed to. Like all soldiers who served as gunners for company commanders, Unteroffizier Langer was well aware of how the opening engagement would play out. Pressing his eye against the primary sight's runner eyecup, the second he saw a brilliant flash off to the right caused by the HOT missile's impact, he cried out, *"FIRING NOW!"*

With that, he, and nine other Leopard 2 gunners loosed a volley that reduced the lead Russian tank company to nothing more than a collection of flaming wrecks, leaving Müller momentarily at a loss for words. It was a state of affairs that lasted but a second. His plan, one he had drilled his company in for months, had played out exactly as he had hoped. Now, however, was not the time to congratulate himself. The shock he expected that the Russian commander across from him was laboring under would not last long. He and his remaining tanks would continue to come. And if they failed to extract revenge for what No. 2 Company, Panzer Battalion 24 had just done, more T-72s belonging to the second echelon would.

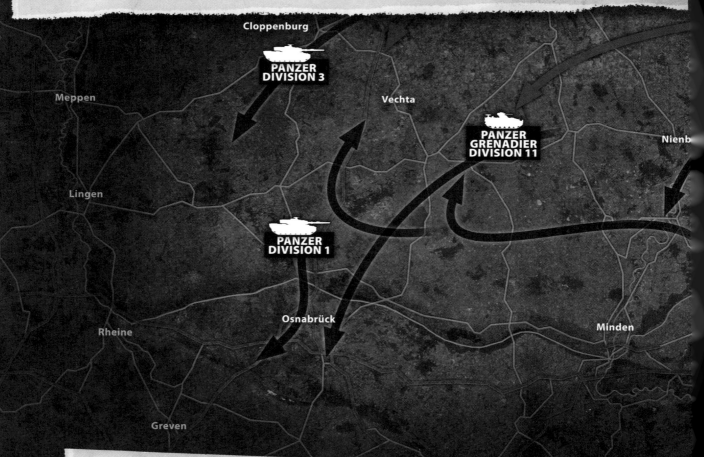

05:30 hrs , 4 August 1985

Having destroyed the lead company, No. 2 Company displaced to its alternate fighting positions southwest of Süpplinegnburg with the exception of 3 Pz Zug which was ordered to take up a position north of the village to block or delay any effort by the enemy to flank the company. They once more halted the attack, before withdrawing again.